Welsh

Cowboys

and Outlaws

DAFYDD MEIRION

y Lolfa

First impression: 2003
© Copyright Dafydd Meirion and Y Lolfa Cyf., 2003

Cover design: Ceri Jones

The *It's Wales* Series, No. 15

ISBN: 0 86243 687 7

Printed on acid-free and partly recycled paper
and published and bound in Wales by
Y Lolfa Cyf., Talybont, Ceredigion SY24 5AP
e-mail ylolfa@ylolfa.com
website www.ylolfa.com
tel (01970) 832 304
fax 832 782

Acknowledgements

Thanks to the following for their help in compiling material for this book:

J Douglas Davies, Llandyfaelog; Margaret Jones Evans, Caernarfon; Gareth Glyn, Llangwyllog; Layton R Green, Pontyclun; Huw Griffith, History Department, University of Wales, Aberystwyth; Gwent Archives; Gwynedd Library Service; Iwan Hughes, Ysgol Maes Garmon; Edna J Jones, Brandon, Vermont; A O Jones, Emsworth, Hamps; Judith Ann Rice-Jones, Colorado; Derek Jones, Wrexham; Robert Lewis, Dolgellau; Margaret Nash, Abercrave; Joe Orfant, Boston, Mass.; Rhys Owen, Y Groeslon; Olwen Owen-Parry, Llandegfan; Bob Priddle, Bridgend; Robert Pugh, Storey Arms; Neil Radnor, Presteigne; David Rees, Lyons, Wisconsin; J Richards, Colorado; Elfyn Schofield, Sully; Angus Snow, Llandinam; The National Library, Aberystwyth; Ellis Thomas, Llangynog; John and Mary Viney, Abergavenny; Eirug Wyn, Y Groeslon

BBC The author wishes to thank BBC Radio Cymru for its permission to use material compiled for the programme *Cymry Gwyllt y Gorllewin* (Producer: Dafydd Meirion) and also BBC 2W for permission to use material from the television programme *Little Big Man* (Producer: Martin Kurzik).

Contents

6. In the Army

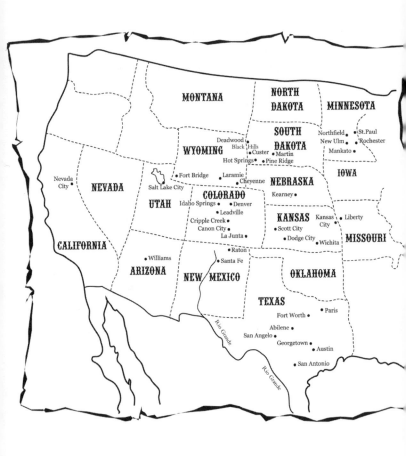

The Wild West

The Background

It is difficult to put an exact figure on how many people from Wales emigrated to the United States. Records show that 80,000 arrived there between 1860 and 1920, but the true figure is probably much higher as the Welsh were very often recorded as being English, which was not true of the Scots and the Irish. For example, in 1880 it was recorded that as many as 83,302 of the inhabitants of the United States had been born in Wales. At the most a quarter of a million left Wales for America, compared to a recorded four and a half million from Ireland.

Over 17% of the Welsh immigrants settled in Pennsylvania with the rest moving out in every direction. A substantial proportion moved west, crossing the prairies and high mountain passes in a fleet of wagons being pulled by horses or more often oxen.

It was a dangerous journey with the weather varying from blazing temperatures to heavy rain and extreme cold. They also faced the wrath of the inhabitants – the native Americans, the so-called Red Indians – who were losing their territories to the white invaders. About 10,000 whites died during these treks westwards, but only 362 were killed by the Indians. The rest were killed by diseases such as typhoid, cholera and smallpox, or succumbed to the wet and cold conditions. The Indians were not the only ones to attack the wagon trains; some were attacked by whites, others by roving bands of Mexicans and renegades.

Decades later, things improved for the whites with the coming of the railways, and where the iron horses stopped for water and provisions small settlements grew, some becoming substantial towns, especially when they became cattle stations. In many of these settlements, the diligent Welsh established their own businesses selling food and clothing, opening hotels and even saloons. Others turned to farming as they had done in the old country. Many became cowboys, miners, railway workers – and many following less respectable professions!

Not every Welsh man or woman in America were chapel people. This is a description of some of the Welsh who settled in Scranton, Pennsylvania:

> *On Main Street there are Welshmen … keeping a bar nearly every other house. If you want … Welsh grogshops, whisky holes, gin mills, rum cellars, go to Lackawanna Avenue, Main Street and Hyde Park. There you will see sons and daughters, husbands and wives, half-drunk all the time, playing silly games, hanging about and singing in Welsh such as that they bring shame to even the half-civilised Irish. If you want lack of respect on the Sabbath, if you want to hear the language of hell … from Welsh mouths, go for half an hour along the streets and into the Welsh saloons in Hyde Park.*
> (Welsh-American newspaper *Y Drych*, 1870)

And this is what the Reverend William Davies Evans in his book *Dros Gyfanfor a Chyfandir* (Over Ocean and Continent) saw in a fair in Kansas:

> *Kansas has passed laws banning the selling and drinking of alcohol in the fair, but some drink on the sly. I saw two, only two, showing their contempt for a town that is temperant. Who were they? Indians? No. Irishmen? No. Germans? No. Yankees? No. Not Welsh, surely? Yes, two Welsh men who had recently arrived from Wales!*

When we think of America, we usually think of the Wild West –

the land of the cowboy, the outlaw and the Indian. These characters became alive to us through books, comics, films and television programmes, and the impression we have is that all these characters were English. But there were many Welsh men and women amongst them, as there were people from other nationalities. Take the cowboy. It is true that most of them spoke English, but only 63% were white men. A quarter were black people and about 12% Mexican with many of the words associated with cowboys coming from Spanish. *Lasso*, the cowboy's rope, and buckaroo from *vaquero* or horseman.

Amongst the white cowboys, there were many nationalities – especially from Germany and Scandinavia. And there were many Celts also; many of them having worked as drovers in the old country, and – so it is said – many willing to work for a lower wage than other nationalities!

Many of the Welsh in the west were honest and hardworking – but just as back home in Wales, there were some unsavoury characters amongst them.

This is the story of some of the Welsh who lived in the Wild West.

1. The Good, the Bad and…

When the Wild West comes to mind, outlaws figure frequently. Men, fast on the draw, with a wide-brimmed hat and the stub of a cheroot cigarette in the corner of the mouth. Men who fired their guns before asking questions. Billy the Kid, John Wesley Hardin, Butch Cassidy and not least – Jesse James and his brother Frank, whose forebears emigrated from Wales. But they were not the only outlaws with Welsh blood in them, there were others just as bad but who did not reach the history books.

Issac Davis – The Malevolent Mormon

It was in 1830 that the Mormons established their first church, in New York. But their habit of having more than wife soon drew attention and they were run out of many a town. By 1843 they had reached Illinois but the following year their leader Joseph Smith was killed by a mob. Brigham Young was then proclaimed their leader and in 1847 he led the Mormons, mainly because of the persecutions in the east, on the historic 1,500 mile journey to Salt Lake City in Utah. Here, initially, they were let alone to carry on with their religion as they saw fit and a flourishing town grew there. Over the years, many returned to their mother country to preach their religion and find converts. Many came to Wales, and one that came under their influence was Isaac Davis.

Issac Davis was the eldest son of Mary Nash and David David of Cydweli, Carmarthenshire. He was raised by his grandparents and apprenticed as a blacksmith. But he came under the influence of the Mormons and began preaching, travelling all over south Wales. About 1846, Issac and his new bride Elizabeth travelled to Liverpool and then to America. They then travelled west by wagon train, eventually arriving in Salt Lake City in Autumn 1849.

But as soon as he arrived there, he fell in love with another woman and although polygamy was practised amongst the Mormons there, it did not receive official approval. He, therefore, had to flee from the area. He travelled from settlement to settlement doing odd jobs but when he was short of cash he was not averse to some spot of thieving, and eventually he fell into bad company.

He had not forgiven those that had driven him from Salt Lake City and some years later he returned to the area with a band of renegade Mormons and Indian half-breeds to raid the settlements.

They attacked isolated farmsteads in daylight and killed innocent farmers, eventually killing over a hundred people. Women were raped and belongings stolen from the wooden cabins. These raids

Mormons on their journey to Salt Lake City

lasted for several months and as there was very little law and order in the province, there was little that could be done to stop the renegades. Eventually a message was sent to the army and a company of soldiers came to the area. Army scouts followed the bandits for days and eventually they caught up with them. But by the time they got word to the rest of the company, the renegades had left the area.

The Mormon renegades used the skills of their fellow Indians to take them over high mountain passes out of reach of the soldiers. They travelled west, eventually splitting up to make it more difficult for the army to follow them.

Davis travelled through Nevada for a few years doing odds jobs on ranches and in shops, and this time succeeding in keeping on the right side of the law. Then, he decided to return to Salt Lake City. On arriving there, he confessed his sins and offered to pay to send the orphans left by the raids a few years earlier east to Missouri and Arkansas.

Once again, he got work doing odd jobs and once again he fell in love! He decided to take another wife, a fifteen year old girl this time, but as he already had two wives he was hauled before the authorities and given a three month prison sentence. After he was released, he went back to his young wife and over the years they had twelve children, with Issac Davies becoming a respectable Mormon and a pillar of the society – a very different life to his wild young days!

The James Brothers – the worst of the Welsh

The most famous of the outlaws of Welsh descent are the brothers Frank and Jesse James. Their great-grandfather, William James (born 1754), was a Baptist minister from Pembrokeshire who emigrated to Pennsylvania. The family later moved west where their father, John James, was a farmer and part-time minister. Frank and Jesse started their bloody careers during the American Civil War when they joined the guerrilla bands of Quantrill and Anderson, killing, burning and looting on behalf of the Confederates. The James Brothers were heroes to the people of the south, but cold-blooded murderers in the eyes of the north.

When the war ended, amnesty was refused to men like the James Brothers who were not members of the official army of the south, and Jesse was shot by soldiers as he tried to give himself up. This is what probably made the boys decide on a career as outlaws and they joined other former guerrillas such as the Younger and Cole brothers stealing from banks, trains and stagecoaches. The brothers, initially at least, saw this as a continuation of the war against the north, and received considerable support from southern folk. Between 1860 and 1881, the James Gang were the most successful outlaws in America, stealing about $200,000 during this period, mainly from banks. Yn 1866, in Liberty, Missouri, the James-Younger Gang undertook the first ever daylight raid on a bank. There were fourteen members in the gang and they stole about $60,000.

By 1875, the Pinkerton Detective Agency had been employed by the railway owners to catch them, and when the agency heard that they were spending a few days home in Kearney, Missouri, they sent a posse of detectives to surround the farmhouse. The brothers had received warning and had left in a hurry, but the detectives did not know this. A device was thrown into the house, a bomb say the family, a flare according to the Pinkertons. It was quickly pushed towards the fireplace where it exploded killing the boys' half-brother and blowing their mother Zerelda's right arm off. This led to even more support for the brothers in Missouri.

One of their most daring raids was in Minnesota in 1876. Their original intention was to raid the bank in Mankato (a town, incidentally, where many people of Welsh descent lived), but during a reconnaissance visit one of the inhabitants recognised Jesse and they had to look for somewhere else to rob. They decided on the bank in Northfield, but this time the inhabitants were ready for them and they attacked the bandits. Three of the outlaws were killed as they came out of the bank and three of the Younger brothers were caught. Three of the inhabitants of Northfield were also killed, including the sheriff and a recent immigrant from Sweden. Frank had been shot in the leg but the brothers managed to escape and galloped out of Northfield with the remains of the gang.

They continued to raid banks and trains until 3 April 1881 when Jesse was shot in the back of the head by Bob Ford, a member of the gang. Although Frank was caught by the authorities, he was found not guilty by the court after a former colonel in the Confederate army vouched for his good character! He spent the rest of his life capitalising on his infamy, welcoming visitors to the family ranch and selling them pebbles from his brother's grave.

According to family tradition, **Issac Morgan** from the Abergavenny/Blaina area rode with the James Gang for a short period. He left Wales for America in the mid 1880s and lived the life of an outlaw there. He later married a Cherokee woman, possibly in Tennessee, after killing her father. He brought his wife Miranda-Jane Redmond (named possibly because of her 'red' skin) and their three children to Abergavenny. But he treated her badly and she returned to the States, without two of the children, in 1905. Morgan later died in the workhouse in Abergavenny. Morgan's 'evidence' of life as an outlaw was kept in a tin box, but as the family wanted nothing to do with him, they were later destroyed.

Many films have been made on the exploits of the James Brothers, including *The Long Riders* which tells the story of the raid on Northfield. Many books have also been written, but they are not the only Welsh outlaws to have their names in print.

Miranda-Jane Redmond

The Cowboy from Cardiff

In 1982, a book called *The Sully Cowboy* was published, based on letters written by Robert Samuel Kenrick from America to his family home in Wales. Kenrick was raised in Sully near Penarth in south Wales but spent a number of years in the Wild West during the late 1880s, early 1890s. He was the son of a sea captain and after leaving school worked as a shipping clerk in Cardiff docks. But he was looking for some adventure and he decided to leave Sully in 1887 and set sail from Liverpool for New York. He then travelled to Kansas where he found work doing odd jobs such as washing dishes in hotels. He met an Englishman there, who was nicknamed Bali, and they became friends.

Kenrick and Bali decided to move west to Denver, Colorado. They were short of money and decided to hitch a free ride on one

A copy of one of Robert Samuel Kenrick's letters to his family where he mentions meeting the outlaws on the train

of the trains. But there were others of the same mind, although they had also decided to rob the train. Someone in one of the stations that they had passed through became suspicious and telegraphed a warning to Denver. There, the sheriff and his men waited on the station platform, guns at the ready. But, somehow, the bandits sensed that there was something wrong and decided to leave the train before reaching Denver.

The two friends decided that it wouldn't be very wise for them to proceed with their train journey, so they also left the train and walked the remaining miles to Denver. When they reached the town, they decided to spend their remaining funds on new clothes and visited one of the numerous stores on the main street. On the way out, they heard a commotion and decided to go and investigate. There they saw the Denver sheriff and his deputies leading the train robbers through the town, each one tied to each other. As they went by, one of the outlaws recognised Kenrick and Bali and shouted a greeting. Immediately, the sheriff pulled out his revolver and aimed it at the two friends. The sheriff took the bundle of new clothes from them as he had jumped to the conclusion that, as they were friends of the train robbers, they must have stolen the clothes. He didn't believe a word they told him and was about to arrest them when Kenrick showed him a letter that he had received from home in Wales. This convinced the sheriff that they were men of good character and they were released. But were they? Were they on better terms with the outlaws than is admitted in his letters?

From Denver, the pair moved to Cheyenne and Laramie where they were hired as cowboys on the HO Ranch. The ranch's foreman was Bill Hanger, a friend of William Frederick Cody, better known as Buffalo Bill. Buffalo Bill was a frequent visitor to the HO to buy horses and Kenrick came to know the buffalo hunter well as he showed the ranch hands his skills with rifle and revolver. Kenrick picked up these skills, and they became very useful to him as he rode the range guarding his boss's cattle.

Not far from the ranch was Pumpkin Buttes, an area well known as a hideout for outlaws, where they hid after raids and buried their booty. One summer, there was a rumour that one gang had been shot up pretty badly during a raid, leaving only two members to flee to the safety of Pumpkin Buttes. Kenrick and some of the other cowboys were in the area looking for stray cattle when they decided to visit the hideout. There was a huge reward for the remaining outlaws but the cowboys were in two minds about handing them over, as they had a strange respect for these bandits. The cowboys found the bandits' hut, but there was nobody there and although they spent some hours looking for the stolen money they had no luck.

There are suggestions in his letters that Kenrick was on good terms with various outlaws. He mentions Butch Cassidy, Kid Donnely and Bill Brady. But although he mixed with the outlaws, he did not forget his upbringing in Wales. In one of his letters, he mentions going to chapel one Sunday, but there was no-one there to play the organ. Kenrick, in his cowboy gear, stood up and walked to the front to play the instrument!

Kenrick returned to Wales in 1892. It is said that he had intended to return to America, but he did not. Had he been warned to stay away because of his friendship with various outlaws? We do not know for sure. Robert Samuel Kenrick died in 1939 and was buried in the churchyard in Sully.

A bullet for Belle Starr's husband

Not everyone in the Wild West was an outlaw; some strived to keep law and order. John T Morris was sheriff of Collins County, Texas, during the 1870s. Amongst the outlaws that plagued the area was James H Reed, leader of a band who plundered all over Missouri, Arkansas, Texas, Arizona, Nevada, California and Oregon. But Reed was better known as the husband of Belle Starr, Queen of the Outlaws.

Reed specialised in horse rustling and robbing stagecoaches. By 1871 Reed and Starr had a business selling horses in Scyene. Belle looked after the business while Reed stole horses in the Indian

Territories which were then sold through the business. This plan worked well as it kept Reed out of the most populous areas where his face was known and where there was a reward for his capture, while Starr kept a 'legitimate' business which gave them a steady income.

But the law was hot on Reed's heels and Sheriff Morris and his deputies had been on his trail for months. They followed him from one dirt town to another, usually arriving a few hours after Reed and Starr had left. Morris learnt that the outlaws were aiming for Paris, Texas, and the lawman took a shortcut over high ground to cut them off. The posse rode through the night and reached Paris on the morning of 6 August 1874. Reed, Starr and two of their men had already arrived and were in the saloon with their horses tethered outside.

Morris ordered his men to surround the saloon, but to keep out of sight. Morris walked on his own into the saloon and immediately saw Reed leaning on the bar. "James H Reed?" he asked.

"Yep," answered Reed.

"I'm arresting you for…" but Sheriff Morris didn't have time to finish his sentence. Reed had gone for his gun, but he wasn't as fast as the lawman and Sheriff Morris fired first. Reed slid to the sawdust floor of the saloon. It was the end of the line for another outlaw, but all in a day's work for Sheriff John T Morris.

There were other Welshmen trying to keep the law in the Wild West. In his book *Y Cymry ac Aur Colorado* (The Welsh and the Gold of Colorado), Eirug Davies mentions Sheriff Jesse Pritchard, originally from the Welsh community of Gomer, Ohio, who 'kept the peace in Central City at one time. Later, he moved to become marshal in Leadville'. In Georgetown, in the same area, John T Davies was the sheriff for a while. Also 'The sheriff in Canon City was W S Jones and the marshal before him was J M Davies … One called Morgan Griffith was the sheriff in Coal Creek for nearly four years, and in another town called Erie, there was a Marshal Tom Williams.'

The Welsh in the Texas Rangers

The Texas Rangers were established in 1835, 150 men whose duties were to keep the Indians at bay and to stop Mexican bandits from crossing the Rio Grande to attack the ranches and steal the cattle. By 1840, they had permanent headquarters in San Antonio and the following year they were amongst the first to use the Colt revolver in the West. The Rangers took part in the American Civil War, mainly guarding the area from attacks from the north, but some officers also joined the Confederate Army.

After the war the Rangers were disbanded but reformed in 1874 due mainly to the increasing attacks from Mexican bandits. By this time the Indians were not a threat as most had signed treaties with the government and had been moved to the reservations. It is said that each Ranger carried two 'bibles'; one was the Holy Bible, the other a list of all the outlaws they were after!

The Rangers continued in existence until August 1935 when they were amalgamated into the State Highway Patrol of Texas. By the 20th century they had exchanged their Colt revolvers for Thompson submachine guns, and on 23 May 1934 two of the Rangers were in south Louisiana as part of a posse that shot 160 bullets through a Ford 8 automobile killing Clyde Barrow and Bonnie Parker – the infamous Bonnie and Clyde.

Frank Jones was born of Welsh extraction in Austin, Texas, and in 1873, when he was 17 years old, he joined the Texas Rangers and became one of its most famous members, taking part in the capture of many outlaws. He was put in D Company and it wasn't long before he took part in his first battle. The Rangers were following a band of Mexicans that had been rustling horses. Trooper Jones and two others were travelling ahead of the rest of the company, following the tracks of the bandits. But they had been seen, and the Mexicans were waiting behind rocks for them.

The bandits were the first to fire, shooting one of the Rangers' horses. The other two jumped off their mounts and dragged their colleague to the shelter of some rocks to avoid the hail of bandit bullets coming in their direction. They could not be certain that the rest of the Rangers could hear the shooting so they decided to settle the bandits on their own. But within a few minutes another of the Rangers went down with a bullet in his head, killing him instantly. The other Ranger had recovered sufficiently to fire back at the bandits whilst Trooper Jones tried to outflank them. Some of the Mexicans were hit but then a bullet through the other Ranger's chest left Jones on his own.

There were only three bandits left by the time Jones got behind them, the others had either been shot or had ran away. Jones jumped from behind a rock and shot two dead immediately and captured the third. He was tied to his horse and led to the rest of the Rangers. Back at base, because of his bravery, Jones was promoted to corporal.

But it was not long before he was promoted to sergeant. One day he was leading seven Rangers on the trail of cattle rustlers. Again, these rustlers found out that Jones was on their heels and they were ready for him. The Rangers were ambushed in a narrow canyon and three of Jones' men were shot dead with the rest being captured.

It was a mistake for the bandits to leave Sergeant Jones alive because, as they were congratulating each other, he snatched one of their rifles and fired wildly towards them, leaving the bandits lying dead in the Texan dirt.

In 1877, Jones was promoted to captain and was given command of D Company. He spent three very busy and bloody years keeping the law in the Lone Star State. Before then, in 1875, an outlaw and ex-Ranger called Scott Cooley had shot John Worley, the deputy sheriff of Mason County. A friend of Cooley had been shot on his way to prison whilst in Worley's charge. Colley blamed the deputy for his friend's death and was gunning for him. This led to a bloody feud in the area which became known as the Mason County War. Dozens were killed and the Rangers were called to stop the fighting, although Cooley escaped.

Years later, Captain Jones saw that Cooley was still on the run and he decided to bring him to justice. But some outlaws saw Jones and decided to ambush him. He was shot in his chest and he fell off his horse and lay in the dirt, blood pouring from his wound. The outlaws were certain that Jones was dead so they took his horse and left him.

Some hours later, Captain Jones came to, and although he was badly wounded he managed to crawl along the desert floor. It got dark and Jones saw a light in the far distance. He crept slowly towards it and when he eventually arrived he saw that they were the three men that had shot him earlier. He waited until they fell asleep, then crept towards them and took one of their rifles. He then lay with his back on a rock for the rest of the night to wait for them to wake up.

When dawn came, the outlaws starred to stir and Captain Jones shouted that he was going to arrest them. One of the outlaws was not very co-operative and he was shot dead. The others, seeing the fate of their friend, held their hands as high as they would go. Jones put the dead man across one horse and tied the other two together and walked them back to the Rangers headquarters in San Antonio. They were tried for cattle rustling and shooting a peace officer and received long sentences. But Scott Cooley was never found.

On 29 June 1893, Captain Frank Jones and four Rangers were on the trail of the Olguin gang – old man Clato, his sons Jesus Maria, Antonio and Pedro and Jesus Maria's son Severio – who had been rustling cattle in Texas. The Rangers followed them for days with the outlaws trying their best to shake them off. But at last the lawmen caught up with them in their hideout on *Tre Jacales* (Three Huts) island in the middle of the Rio Grande. The wooden huts were surrounded and a battle started, which raged for some hours, but the Mexicans, apart from Clato, managed to escape.

The Rangers left him there and went back to their camp but after a few miles they saw two riders on the horizon. They decided to follow them and saw that they were part of Olguin's band. The rustlers saw them and galloped away, but the Rangers caught up with them and within a hundred yards the Mexicans reached the ruins of some buildings and started shooting at the lawmen. There were at least a dozen men in the ruins and the Rangers had been led into a trap! The Rangers leapt off their horses, and using them as shields, fired at the gang. Jones was the first to be hit, with a bullet through his thigh. Corporal Kirchner tried to help him but Jones was shot again, this time in his chest, and he ordered the corporal to go back. Jones tried to continue the fight, but eventually he fell to the ground, dead. Such was the ferocity of the bandits' firing that the Rangers had to retreat, leaving their captain's body where it had fell. He was 37 years old.

The Rangers had without realising crossed the border into Mexico, where they had no jurisdiction. They therefore decided to return to their camp. A request was made to the authorities in Juarez state to go and fetch Captain Jones' body, but they were refused. Numerous diplomatic messages were sent to Mexico City and at last President Diaz agreed, mainly because both he and Jones were freemasons! Amongst the men who went to fetch Captain Frank Jones' body was Sergeant John Reynolds Hughes.

John Reynolds Hughes was raised on a ranch in Cambridge, Illinois, and as a Ranger he came across men such as John Wesley Hardin, Pancho Villa, Billy the Kid, Butch Cassidy, Pat Garrett and Judge Roy Bean. Hughes's grandparent had left Wales for America and his father, Thomas Hughes, had visited Wales twice to see his relatives.

By the middle of the 1870s, Hughes was working on a ranch in Oklahoma which was being pestered by cattle rustlers. But one day, after a substantial raid, Hughes decided to go after the rustlers. He followed them for days, over rivers, deserts and mountains until he caught up with them near woodland on the banks of a river where the rustlers had stopped to water the cattle. There were six in the band under the leadership of the notorious Nig Goombi. Hughes galloped into their midst, a gun blazing in each hand. Goombi was shot dead but the others escaped. The dead rustler was tied across a horse and taken back with the cattle to the ranch.

By 1877, Hughes had reached Texas and a year later he had bought his own farm. Once again he was pestered by rustlers and one again he decided to go after them. He caught up with them in the wilds of New Mexico when they were about to lie down for the night. Once again Hughes charged into them, his guns blazing. When the smoke cleared, two rustlers were dead and another was wounded and taken to the nearest sheriff's office.

But the rustling continued, so in 1887 Hughes travelled to Georgetown, Texas, and joined the Texas Rangers. He reasoned that if he was going to fight rustlers all his life, he might as well get paid for it!

By 1893, after many a shoot-out with rustlers and outlaws,

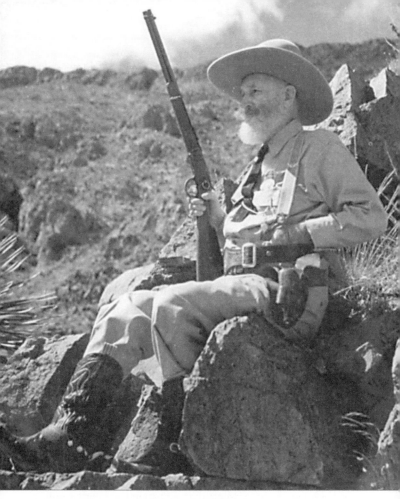

Captain John Reynolds Hughes, some years after he retired

Hughes had been promoted to sergeant in D Company, Frontier Division. Some months later, Captain Frank Jones was killed by Olguin and his band and Hughes took over as captain.

One of Hughes' first tasks as captain was to find those responsible for Jones' death. He led his men down to the Rio Grande and he caught up with the bandits one by one. Hughes heard that Olguin and his son was in a cantina in one of the small border towns. The Rangers travelled as quickly as possible to the town and surrounded the building. Hughes shouted an order for the bandits to throw out their weapons and come out with their hands in the air. But they did not take kindly to this, and came out with their guns blazing – one through the door, the other through a window. Seconds later, both lay dead on the dusty street, their guns still in their hands.

Hughes did not always take his men with him and he would sometimes track outlaws on his own. It was on his own that he decided to go after Juan Perales who had crossed the Rio Grande for some killing and thieving. Hughes left early one morning with enough provisions for a week and a piece of paper with Perales' details on it. He wandered from one dirt town to another, asking if anyone had seen the Mexican. Everyone had heard of him but had no idea where he was. Hughes heard that someone had been shot dead in one of the nearby villages and he decided to go and investigate. The murderer was of the same description as Perales but he had a day's start on Hughes. Hughes went in the direction that the bandit had been last seen, and eventually came across tracks in the sand and after a few hours tracking came across a sombrero behind a rock. He dismounted and crept slowly around it. There, having his siesta, was Perales. Hughes pulled his gun and kicked the bandit's legs to wake him up. Perales went for his gun, but when he saw the Ranger he soon dropped it and surrendered with a smile on his face.

Over the years Captain John R Hughes was responsible for bringing dozens of rustlers and outlaws to justice in the wild lands bordering Mexico. In 1915, when he was 60 years old, he decided to retire. He died in Austin, Texas, in 1946 having reached 91 years of age.

The Preacher amongst the drunken Mexicans

It wasn't only the sheriffs, marshals and Rangers that tried to tame the West. Many preachers travelled west to try and save the souls of the inhabitants – with only limited success. In 1881, the Reverend William Davies Evans decided to visit the Western states, travelling from town to town in a stagecoach and staying, where possible, with fellow Welshmen.

But there was no Welsh welcome in La Junta, Colorado, when he arrived there on 29 November 1881. That evening, while waiting for the stagecoach, the Reverend Evans and his fellow travellers went to a local cantina. The reverend had some coffee whilst the rest of the passengers had a beer. But not everyone were so moderate in their drinking habits and at midnight four drunken Mexicans staggered into the cantina. They ordered some whisky and sat by the only stove that was set in the middle of the cantina, thus keeping the warmth from everyone else in the room.

The Mexicans started arguing amongst each other who was the best shot. Suddenly they all stood up and waved their pistols above their heads. The preacher and the other passengers moved back and put their backs against the cantina wall with their eyes on the door ready to get out. The Mexicans had by now decided to start shooting at the earthen pots that were on the cantina walls. Fortunately, the stagecoach guard came in with his shotgun at the ready. He ordered the Mexicans to drop their guns and leave the cantina. Each one obeyed and left the building and the passengers could hear their horses galloping down the town's dusty road. The Reverend W D Evans was more than glad to leave La Junta.

Annie Ellis – lodging lady to the lawmen

It wasn't just men that ventured west; there were of course many women amongst them and one of these was Annie Ellis who was born in Dolgellau in 1845. She was thirteen years old when she arrived in America with her older brother who was supposed to look after her. But when they reached Kansas City he left her on her own. She was seen wandering the streets and was taken in by the authorities who put her in the care of a charitable organisation until she was 19 years old.

She then married David Rule, an itinerant carpenter who was twenty-five years older than her. Around 1870, they arrived in Abilene, Kansas, but they did not have much of a married life as her husband spent most of his time working for the army and travelling from one fort to another. In 1871 Annie became friendly with Wild Bill Hickock who found work for her in an eating house. Eventually Annie saved enough money to open a lodging house in Wichita and amongst her customers there were Wyatt Earp and Bat Masterson. But the lodging house was not very successful, and she closed it down and moved to Dodge City. During this time, her husband was working in Kansas City and one day he went to the bank to get some money. He

Wyatt Earp stayed in Annie Ellis' lodging house in Wichita, Kansas

took the money back to his hotel, but later that night thieves broke into his room, killed him and stole his money. At that time Annie was not working and she was left penniless.

But she remarried, this time to a rich rancher called George Anderson. She was given money by her new husband to buy land from Bat Masterson and also to open another lodging house and restaurant on Second Avenue, Dodge City. There, some of the famous and infamous characters of the period came to stay and eat, including Wyatt Earp, Bat Masterson, Luke Short and Bill Tilghman. One time, Earp and one of his deputies – Bill Tilghman – had fallen out, and Earp was out looking for him. Tilghman borrowed one of Annie's dresses and escaped from the irate lawman!

Annie's businesses prospered as more people moved west. The settlements changed from one-horse towns into prosperous settlements with many shops, hotels and saloons. Annie Ellis Rule Anderson died in 1931, a fairly rich woman. According to Annie, the sheriffs and marshals of the period such as Earp and Masterson were "gentlemen … they gave their enemies a chance".

2. There's gold in them thar hills...

During the 19th century, thousands trekked west hoping to make their fortunes in the gold and silver mines. Naturally, there were many Welshmen amongst them, several with experience of mining in the old country. Camps were established wherever finds were made and some of these camps became substantial settlements, most of them lawless and dangerous. There was more violence in these settlements than in other towns in the West, because they attracted some men who were more interested in stealing a miner's hard-earned gold rather than in prospecting themselves.

Candelaria, Nevada, established in 1865, was a typical miners' town. Not only were two newspapers published there, but it also had ten saloons, six eating houses and two hotels, and in the area known as Pickhandle Gulch there were ten prostitutes offering comfort to the miners twenty-four hours a day! Shootings were a common occurrence with many being killed. But you could always plead self-defence and over a period of over forty years, only seven were charged with murder, but none of them were taken in front of a court of law.

Most towns did not have a sheriff or marshal to keep the peace, and if they did have one, he wouldn't last long. For example, Tin Cup, Colorado, had four sheriffs between 1881 and 1883; three were shot dead within a few days of starting their job and the fourth had to be taken to a mental hospital!

In the saloons

One of the thousands that were drawn west to chance their luck was **Edward Davies**. Davies had been working in the Nant Bwlch yr Heyrn mines near Llanrwst and was well-known in the area as a gifted musician – a pianist and choir leader. About 1891 he emigrated to America and joined the Gold Rush in Colorado, hoping that his wife and children would follow him there after he struck lucky, but they decided to stay in Wales. Edward doesn't seem to have found much gold, but at least he had his

Edward Davies and his medals before leaving for America

musical talents to earn some money. The last his family heard of him was that he was a piano player in one of the numerous saloons in the area.

Another Welshman that entertained the saloon regulars was **John G Jones** who was born in Bethesda, north Wales, in 1869 and emigrated to America when young. He was in the Cripple Creek area of Colorado by the early 1890s. John or Jack as he was known to his family travelled from one saloon to another with two other men and a stage show. The two men would 'read' the audience's minds whilst Jack entertained them by singing.

Jones had not written to his mother home in Wales for several weeks and she became worried. As she was a religious woman, she contacted the Salvation Army to ask them to get a message to Jack

Le Munyon,
13 Park Drive South.
Great Falls, Mont.

Photograph of John G Jones, aged 22 or 23, taken in Great Falls, Montana

in Cripple Creek. In no time, the Army found the saloon where he was working and one evening sang outside, "Dear Jack, your mother is waiting to hear from you"! After the embarrassment, Jones would write regularly home to his mother. He even started going to Salvation Army meetings as he had fancied one of the girls there. He tried to persuade her to go out with him, but she had no interest in a saloon entertainer and slapped him across his face for his impudence. That was the last time that he ventured to one of their meetings!

The trio did well and had saved a substantial amount of money, but one of the mind readers went to the Kentucky Derby and lost all the money on horses! Jones moved back to New York where he became a successful financier and died there in 1956.

Daniel W Williams and the Miners' Courts

Daniel W Williams left Penmaen, Monmouthshire, for America and arrived in Bannack, Montana, in July 1863 with the intention of making his fortune in the gold and silver mines. On the way there, he called in Rock Island, Illinois, then went on to Kearney, Fort Laramie and Sweetwater in a wagon train consisting of twenty men and one woman in nine wagons being pulled by horses and mules. During the journey they were nearly killed by Indians and had to be rescued by the army.

After leaving the wagon train, Williams headed for the miners' town of Bannack, Montana. Gold had been found in Grasshopper Creek in 1862 and the town had risen overnight. There was no law in Bannack as the sheriff was in cahoots with many of the outlaws. It is said that at least one man was shot or stabbed each night in Syrus Skinner's saloon. At one time, Bannack was the capital of Montana, but there is little left there now apart from a few ruined buildings. When Williams arrived in 1863, one of the first he met was Haze Lyons with whom he became friendly, but at the time he knew nothing of Lyons' background.

Lyons was a member of Sheriff Henry Plummer's gang which attacked stagecoaches in the area. Plummer was an outlaw who found nothing wrong in wearing the five-pointed star, but in the last few months of 1863 his chief deputy, a man called Dillingham, became suspicious. One night, Dillingham was patrolling the streets of Bannack, checking the doorways and alleyways but at the far end of the street Lyons, gun in hand, was waiting for him. When the deputy was within fifty yards of him, Lyons jumped out with his gun blazing. The deputy fell to the ground – dead.

But it didn't take long for Lyons to be caught. A posse galloped out of town after him and within a few days another of Bannack's deputies arrested him and brought him back to town. He was dragged to court and there, in his defence, he read out his last letter to his mother, an act that brought tears to the eyes of the hard-living miners. "Give him a *** horse and let him return to his *** mother," cried one of the miners and Lyons was freed. But he did not see his mother; on a cold morning on January 14th 1864, vigilantes caught up with him and hanged him from the nearest tree.

Daniel Williams did not stay long in Bannack as he had heard that that there was better luck to be had in Alder Gulch. Two months before Williams arrived, gold had been found there, and already between a thousand and 1,500 men had arrived there, living in tents and holes in the ground on a strip of land ten miles long. The settlement grew to be Virginia City, a town that eventually became home to 25,000 people. By today, only about five hundred live there but it is one of the main tourist areas of Nevada.

But Williams had no luck there and he moved on to Bachelor Gulch. He was not a good judge of men's characters as he met another of Plummer's men, George Ives, there. Ives was asking around who had struck lucky as it was his intention to steal their gold from them. At first his gang was successful, but they were soon caught and were dragged to Nevada City by a gang of miners fed up with their thieving and killing. Williams was with his fellow miners in the court in Nevada City to see justice being done. Such was the skill and ability of the young prosecuting lawyer that the bandits could see that there was no escape. At the back of the court, Williams heard one of the bandits' friends, who was a noted gambler, whisper, "We'll fix the guy." Williams told the rest of the miners what he had heard and they helped the young lawyer to get out of court and to Virginia City unharmed. Ives and his fellow outlaws were dragged out of court and hanged.

As there was very little law in these parts, the miners would set up their own courts. Outlaws were not the only ones dragged in front of these courts. One evening, Williams and his fellow miners were called to hear the case of a man who was continually drunk and who beat his wife. She worked hard washing clothes while he spent her money on whisky. The wife showed her bruises to the court and it did not take the miners long to find the man guilty. There was no gaol in Bachelor Gulf then, but the miners had two methods of punishing villains – hanging them or running them out of town. In this case, they chose the second option including forty lashes, but before the whip was raised some of the man's friends attacked the miners and in the scuffle he got away and fled to the mountains.

In another court, Daniel Williams was present when a defendant pulled a gun out and aimed it at a miner that was testifying against him. "Speak another word and you'll be a dead man," said the defendant. The miners in the courtroom pulled out their guns and pointed them at him. He soon dropped his gun and after he was found guilty was run out of town.

But Welshmen also found themselves on the wrong side of the law. Here is an extract from *Y Cymry ac Aur Colorado* (The Welsh and the Gold of Colorado) by Eirug Davies:

> *In the spring of 1874 some of the Welsh of Spanish Bar got into trouble in Idaho Springs and they were given a warning to keep away. The Welshmen would not take this warning, and therefore, on a Saturday night a dozen of them went to the village. They came face to face with their enemies and both sides decided that they would choose one to fight on their behalf. The Welshmen chose Evan S Evans and the Germans a man called Rueder. But after having gone outside and taken their clothes off, the German refused to fight. This led to a scuffle and the Welshman John Hughes Ffordd Deg was stabbed by the Germans.*

Here is another extract from the book:

> *Amongst the three that escaped on Sunday from the Canon City gaol was, unfortunately, a Welshman. We hope that William Parry during his flight to safety, will remember the honour of his nation by keeping out of any more trouble.*

3. The Cowboys and the Ranchers

Many of the Welsh who emigrated to America came from an agricultural background; some had enough money to buy their own ranches, others became cowboys. There was a particular mystique attached to the life of the free American farmer. He was regarded as the only true independent man. Welsh farmers emigrated to seek broader and more fertile acres of which they could be freeholders and not have to pay rent. A host of farm labourers dreamed that they, too, could in turn save enough money to buy land after working for a time as hired hands in America.

The word *ranch* comes from the Spanish *rancho*, meaning 'persons feeding in company'. Most of the ranches bred cattle and there were three types of these animals – the longhorns, Herefords and crossbreeds. The longhorns were the most numerous up until the end of the 1880s when Hereford cattle were taken west (more on this later). The longhorns had originated in the Andalusia area of Spain, brought over by the Spanish and many having escaped from the ranches roamed wild on the plains. Although they were not particularly good for their meat, they were tough animals able to live in barren country. Without any money to start with, many of the whites became prosperous ranchers simply by catching these animals. Another disadvantage of the longhorns was that they were ill-tempered and vicious, and Herefords and cross Longhorn-Durham or Longhorn-Hereford became more common as they were much easier to manage. In order that there was enough land for the cattle to graze, the buffaloes were killed and driven from their habitats and with the coming of the railways these magnificent beasts were almost killed to extinction.

Most of the lands were in the hands of a few powerful men, many of them living in the east and some even in Europe. Hundreds of cowboys worked on these vast ranches. In the early days, it was possible for a cowboy to start his own small ranch as there was a tradition that he could keep his boss's mavericks – calves without mothers. But as land became scarcer this custom ended. Nevertheless, it was still a temptation to take these mavericks and many became rustlers and were hunted down by men hired by the big ranchers.

Others came to the West to breed horses, usually selling them to the army. Once again, many started off by catching wild mustangs with their *lassos* or *lariats.*

Sheep farmers soon followed and they started to compete with the cattle ranchers for grass. If the sheep had got there first, there would be no grass left for the cattle. Fences would keep cattle away from grass, but they were useless against sheep. Cattle would refuse to go where sheep had been grazing as they didn't like their smell and to many cowboys, sheep were not 'proper' animals – only cattle and horses were supposed to be in the Wild West! But their biggest objection was that sheep farmers were recent immigrants to the area, with many of them coming from Scotland, the Basque Country and Mexico. The ranchers would threaten the farmers, killing their sheep and burning their hay, and even sometimes killing the shepherds. It was much easier to become a sheep farmer as the animals were cheaper to buy, and they went to market quicker, and the farmer would get his money back sooner. They also needed less men to look after them.

The plains were vast. Much, much larger than anything back home in Wales. This is how the Reverend William Davies Evans (the preacher who met the drunken Mexicans in La Junta) describes the plains in his book *Dros Gyfanfor a Chyfandir* (Over Ocean and Continent):

Land! Land! Land! as far as the eye can see in every direction. An
unending sea of land! Yes, more than the sea by far. The sea
disappears. The horizon looks so near; but on these huge prairies,
they reach far, far to somewhere. It is amazing how anyone could
think of a world as large as this. Looking at these plains causes one
to say, "Enough". Looking as far as this, one does not have the
strength to look further. The extremities disappear, not
unceremoniously at once as does the sea, but gradually, gently,
lovingly dissolve.

Rancher George Price and the Buffalo Hunters

One that prospered as a rancher by dealing with some of the most
prominent characters of the West was George Price. His father,
Morris Price, had left Wern Goch Farm, Abaty Cwm Hir, Rhayadr,
Powys, for America and travelled on to Big Rock, Kane County,
Illinois, where he started a small ranch. He became one of the
biggest ranchers in the area and many places were named after the
family. When George was young, the family left Big Rock and
bought a three thousand acre ranch in Mead County, South
Dakota, in the foothills of the Black Hills. There he bred horses for
the cavalry, with soldiers coming to his ranch to buy the animals. As
Wild Bill Hickock and Buffalo Bill worked as army scouts in the
area they were frequent visitors to the ranch.

Another visitor was Martha Jane Cannary or Calamity Jane who
had joined the army pretending to be a boy. She was put in charge
of the mules, until she was found out and thrown out of the army.
She later married Wild Bill and they had a child, but Hickock was
shot dead on 2 August 1876. Cannary remarried but the marriage
was not a success and in August 1893 she joined Buffalo Bill's
Wild West Show.

George Price became a rich man, but life was not without its troubles. He and his men had to cope with not only the weather, prairie fires, Indians and rustlers, but he also had his share of bad luck. One of his sons, Vernon, was killed while out riding. He and a young Indian were galloping through a nearby forest when Vernon turned round to throw a walnut at his friend, but he didn't see the branch ahead of him and he was struck in his head and killed.

Buffalo Bill used to buy horses from George Price

Wild Bill Hickock, I presume?

Another Welshman who came across Wild Bill Hickock was John Rowlands who was raised in a workhouse in St Asaph near Denbigh. He emigrated to America, changed his name to H M Stanley and later became famous as an African Explorer and the man who greeted Livingstone with the words, "Dr. Livingstone, I presume?" Before venturing to Africa, he spent many years in America writing articles for many newspapers and magazines. One of these articles – for the *Weekly Missouri Democrat* of St Louis – was an interview with James B (Wild Bill) Hickock in 1867:

> *Stanley: I say Bill, how many white men have you killed, to your certain knowledge?"*
> *Hickock: I would be willing to take my oath on the Bible tomorrow that I have killed over a hundred.*

Wild Bill went on to say how he killed his first white man:

I was twenty-eight years old when I killed the first white man, and if ever a man deserved killing he did. He was a gambler and counterfeiter, and I was in a hotel in Leavenworth City then, and seeing some loose characters around, I ordered a room, and as I had some money about me, I thought I would go to it. I had lain some thirty minutes on the bed, when I heard some men at my door. I pulled my revolver and bowie-knife and held them ready, but half concealed, still pretending to be asleep. The door was opened, and five men entered the room. They whispered together 'let us kill the son of a bitch; I'll bet he has got money'.

Gentlemen, that was a time – an awful time. I kept perfectly still until just as the knife touched my breast, I sprang aside and buried mine in his heart, and then used my revolver on the others right and left. Only one was wounded, besides the one killed; and then gentlemen, I dashed through the room and rushed to the fort, procured a lot of soldiers, came to the hotel and captured the whole gang of them, fifteen in all. We searched the cellar and found eleven bodies buried there – men who were murdered by those villains. Would you have done the same? That was the first man I killed, and I never was sorry for that yet.

As a journalist, H M Stanley travelled with the US Cavalry in Missouri and Kansas where they fought battles with the Indians. On 21 October 1867 Stanley was in Medicine Lodge Creek, Kansas, when 7,000 Indians of the Kiowa, Commanche and Arapaho tribes came to sign a treaty with the American government. The Indians, in return, were given lands on the Red and Washita rivers.

Charles Samuel Thomas and the cattle drives

Charles Samuel Thomas left Llangynog on the slopes of the Berwyn mountain in north Wales in 1878 for America. He travelled to Cleveland and then on to Denver, Colorado, where he found work with a company selling meat. By 1880 he had reached Cheyenne where he worked for a company breeding cattle and selling their hides. The company also sold meat to the army at Fort Laramie and bought furs from the Indians. As part of his duties, he would go into the mountains to meet the Indians to buy the furs. One time, he was riding through a small forest when Indians attacked him. He pulled out his revolvers and shot at them, but one managed to throw a tomahawk which hit him on his head. Thomas fell off his horse and although blood was streaming down his face managed to keep shooting and the Indians in the end gave up. When Thomas got up he saw that he had killed five Indians. He caught his horse

Charles S Thomas on a poster when he stood for county commissioner of Laramie County

PLEASE VOTE FOR

CHARLES THOMAS

FOR COUNTY COMMISSIONER.

and galloped back to the safety of Fort Laramie.

Years later, his brother John joined him and they bought a ranch in the area and within a short time they had four thousand acres of land. In 1884, the brothers bought two and half thousand head of longhorn cattle in Mexico and drove them across the Rio Grande with the help of Texas Rangers to guard them from Indians and rustlers. The Rangers were with them as far as La Junta, Colorado, where a number of Thomas' men came to meet them and helped them get the cattle to the end of the journey in Wyoming.

Another time, they bought twenty thousand sheep in Oregon and drove them across country on a journey that took six months for the ten men and three chuck-wagons. Indians watched them from the nearby hills and the men rode backwards and forwards with their guns at the ready in case they were attacked. There were many natural obstacles on the journey – mountain ranges and many wide rivers where the sheep had to be pushed into the water to swim across.

Life was not easy for the brothers or their workers. The winters were harsh and in order for the men to be able to shelter from the elements while tending the animals, dugouts were built into the sides of hills and a bed and cooking equipment placed there. The Thomas brothers visited the dugouts every week bringing fresh supplies. The brothers' situation was not comfortable, initially, either. Their home in the first few years was a dirt hut, but as things improved they built a wooden ranch house and life became easier.

One time, some of the Thomas men came across an old Indian and took him back to the ranch with them. Soon One-eyed Jack became part of the family and lived in a cabin at the back of the house. One-eyed Jack taught the Thomas brothers' children to hunt and trap and when he died he was buried near the ranch.

But it wasn't just the Indians and the weather that made life difficult for the brothers; they also had trouble with some of their fellow whites. Fencing and sheep caused much trouble. Fences had been cut by a neighbour to drive sheep to their sections to graze on the Thomas' land. On one occasion, the Thomas men dragged barbed wire from their saddles, entwining the sheep and cutting them up badly.

Another time Charles and John Thomas and six of their men were digging a ditch on their property. They were setting ties up on one end in the ditch to form a shelter for their cattle when someone shot at them. The bullet hit one of the posts they were setting. Charles Thomas went to the two-wheeled cart they had, got hold of his 47-70 Winchester, mounted his horse and rode around looking for snipers. He couldn't find any so he and the men returned to the ranch. However, a few days later someone shot and killed one of the Thomas riders. A couple of days later two of their neighbour's herders were found shot to death at their wagon. The local deputy sheriff came to the ranch to investigate but no-one was arrested.

The First Herefords

Many Welsh people left a permanent mark on the West's agriculture; no-one less than the Radnors of Presteigne in Powys

Thomas Arthur Radnor's men in Kansas

who were the first to import to America Hereford cattle or white-faces as they were known. Thomas Arthur Radnor took a Hereford bull called Radnor 1 with a handful of cows to Scott City, Kansas, in the 1870s. Up until then, the longhorns had dominated the scene. The Herefords did not receive much of a welcome at first, but in time they took over from the longhorns as they were much better at producing meat.

The story of the introducing of Hereford cattle to the West is to be had in the film *The Rare Breed* with James Stewart, but there is no reference there to the Welsh, apart from the fact that the owner of the white-faced bull is called Mrs Evans!

The Texas Shepherd

Another who tried to improve his situation was William Davies of Cwm Farm, Bedwas, Monmouthshire. He made his money in America breeding not cattle, but sheep. His brother John was already in America where, after working as a lumberjack, he had bought a small hotel in Minnesota. Davies was only in Texas for about twelve years but he had saved enough money to come home to Wales to run a tavern and build a large house for himself and his wife.

Davies was twenty-four years old when he left home in July 1879. He landed in New York a month later

A photograph of William Davies taken in San Angelo in 1889

and aimed for Wisconsin where his brother lived. But the life of a lumberjack did not appeal to him so he travelled two and a half thousand miles in a fortnight to Fort Worth, Texas. There he found work on the Texas Pacific Railroad and, according to a letter he sent home to his mother, managed to save forty dollars in a four months. But he added that it took twice as much determination to stay away from temptation as it did home in Wales! He does not mention if he succumbed to these temptations or not!

Two months later he had travelled two hundred miles to San Angelo where he found work as a shepherd. There were nearly three and a half thousand sheep there and it was Davis' job to travel with them in a small wagon, sleeping under the stars, even in winter. He suffered greatly by a fever brought on by the cold weather and he would take quinine to make himself better. The food wasn't too good either. He complained in his letters to his mother than it was impossible to buy cheese in Texas – and he having been brought up on Caerphilly cheese! One time, when food was scarce, Davies had to boil frogs and grasshoppers to make a stew!

But looking after someone else's sheep didn't appeal much to Davies, and he borrowed money from his mother to buy a thousand sheep in San Antonio, Texas. To guard his sheep from the wolves – two-legged as well as four-legged – he carried with him a pistol and rifle wherever he went. Even so, he had not forgotten his upbringing in Wales, and his mother used to regularly send him copies of the Welsh religious paper *Seren Cymru*.

But everyone in Texas were not of the same character and he notes in his letters home that although most of the men – be they shepherds or cowboys – worked hard, once they had been paid they headed for the nearest town and spent all their money in the saloons. After spending every cent, they had to return to work to make some more money and the vicious circle started once again.

Davies saw many a shoot-out – or at least heard them – he says in his letters. Most of the trouble started in the saloons after much drinking, and once the shooting started, everyone would jump out of the saloon doors. When he was asked after returning to Wales whether men shot each other, his reply was, "No, not each other. They usually shot other people. They were too drunk to shoot straight and they usually shot innocent bystanders!"

But it wasn't just drink that caused men to start shooting at each other. One night, Davies was sitting under a tree in front of a fire guarding his sheep during a journey from Frio County to Fort Concho. In the distance he could see, silhouetted against the setting sun, men on horseback coming towards him, but as they came nearer he lost sight of them. Suddenly, he heard horses galloping towards him and seconds later a bullet narrowly missed him. He jumped behind the tree to shelter from any more bullets, but by now it was too dark to shoot back. There was considerable bad feeling between the sheep farmers and the ranchers in the area. The ranchers were the first in the territory and they continually complained that sheep were ruining the cattle's grass. As in Wales, it was difficult to stop sheep from wandering onto a neighbour's land, but here there were no fences, walls or hedges as there are in Wales. This led, as in the case of the Thomas brothers, to fighting between both sides. It seems that a local rancher had not been too happy to have Davies and his sheep near his land and that they had shot at him to warn him away.

Within nine years, Davies owned over three thousand acres in Texas, but he still had *hiraeth* for the old country and in 1891 he returned to Monmouthshire and built a large house, Nantgoch, with the proceeds of the Texas sheep.

Owen Roscomyl – the Welsh Cowboy

Owen Roscomyl was a Welshman who loved the typical life of the cowboy. In 1880, when he was sixteen years old, Arthur Owen Vaughan or Owen Roscomyl, fled on a ship from Porthmadog to America. He then moved west and worked as a cowboy in Colorado, Wyoming, Montana and California. In Montana, he was caught up in the Range Wars and in a series of letters home to his family he tells of his exploits on the range:

4th July, 1880, Middle Kiowa, Colorado

I have exchanged the garments of civilisation for some not of English style, pants made of grizzly skin, tanned and with the hair on; instead of boots, rawhide moccasins, my hat and blue shirt hold good yet; no-one would think I was the most verdant of tenderfeet to see me.

This is a bully life, riding all day. Just before sundown we camped and unsaddled, hobbling the horses we turn them loose. After supper we spread our beds (generally consisting of blankets and skins), and then turn in with the silvery moon for a lamp. We snooze till the light begins to show in the east. When we rise, we take up our beds and walk as far as the wagon into which we pitch them. Then we catch our horses, breakfast and by four o'clock we are off on circles. By noon we are back in camp with the cattle. We take dinner and then the fun begins for there is more hard, mad riding done, in cutting out wild cattle from a herd of 4-5,000 head, than anywhere else in the world.

The other day I was off on a circle when I saw a herd of wild horses. I got behind the herd before they knew it and, lariat in hand, dashed at them. I marked out a black stallion whose fine form and glossy coat made a perfect picture and dashing thro' the rear of the flying herd, I flung my rawhide rope so that it fell on his neck. He made a wild plunge but he was fast to my saddle horn. When the herd had passed I jerked him off his feet and before he could run, I took the rope from his neck and mounting my horse drove him into camp.

We now have to keep our shooting irons loaded and to keep our eyes skinned for the Indians. Two or three years ago Vittorio and his Apaches were living in peace on the barren reservation in New Mexico. The whites removed him without any apparent reason to San Carlos where his people sickened and died. When the chief saw his tribe melting like snow he marched the remnant back to their old home vowing he would never leave it again and he has been fighting ever since. He is helped by Comanches, Navajos, Zinees and Utes. The various tribes have had a pow wow so they may unite any moment and plunge the whole frontier into a bloody disastrous war. I may help to take a herd of cattle either to the Republican River or to the Ute Reservation and in either case the Indians will attempt to take the herd of cattle from us. Then there will be fun for we shall defend the herd and our scalps.

8th August, 1880, the Republican River, Colorado

About midnight … I was awakened by a noise resembling that of a herd of cattle stampeding. Jumping up I looked for my horse but couldn't clap eyes on him. Looking up to the sky I saw a fearful sight. The glare of a fire mingled with huge black clouds of smoke told me that the prairie was on fire. I had camped in a little hollow so that my fire should not be seen on the prairie. I saw about a mile away a vast sea of fire. Horses, cattle and wild animals were fleeing before the fire. I ran back to my fire and espied my horse, saddled him like lightning and was off. I got to the top of the next hill, I

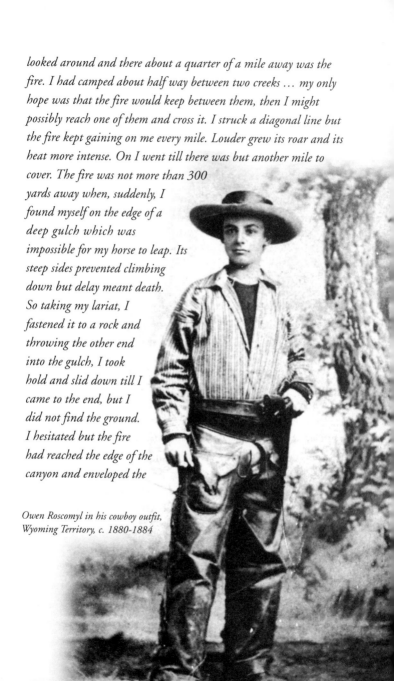

looked around and there about a quarter of a mile away was the fire. I had camped about half way between two creeks ... my only hope was that the fire would keep between them, then I might possibly reach one of them and cross it. I struck a diagonal line but the fire kept gaining on me every mile. Louder grew its roar and its heat more intense. On I went till there was but another mile to cover. The fire was not more than 300 yards away when, suddenly, I found myself on the edge of a deep gulch which was impossible for my horse to leap. Its steep sides prevented climbing down but delay meant death. So taking my lariat, I fastened it to a rock and throwing the other end into the gulch, I took hold and slid down till I came to the end, but I did not find the ground. I hesitated but the fire had reached the edge of the canyon and enveloped the

Owen Roscomyl in his cowboy outfit, Wyoming Territory, c. 1880-1884

rock to which I had fastened my lariat. An instant later the rope broke, sending me down to the bottom.

I must have been knocked senseless for the next thing I remember it was dark and silent. I lay there till morning came. I got up and tried to walk slowly and at last got to the mouth of the canyon and got up to the flat where I had ridden the night before. As far as I could see there was nothing but the blackness and desolation and I had lost all I possessed – horse, saddle, rifle, blanket, and was 50 miles from camp with nothing but revolver and knife.

I resolved to stay where I was a day or so. I killed a prairie dog and made breakfast. About noon a bunch of cattle came thro'. Their owner was taking them near the same place I was bound for and offered to take me along if I would help drive. I accepted his offer and got back to camp in a few days.

January 1881, Wyoming Territory

I was with my boss out on the prairie when I spoke about my wages. We got quarrelling and he drew his pistol and fired at me, but I made my horse rear. The bullet struck my horse, I jumped from the saddle just in time to avoid the second bullet, the third did no serious damage, but in replying to his kind attentions I plugged him in the shoulder. Then he dropped his pistol and turning his horse he scooted. I fired at him again, hitting him in the leg and also wounding his horse, but he managed to get away. I stayed there till the afternoon when a drove of cattle came along bound for the Laramie Plains via Cheyenne. The boss hired me to go along to Laramie.

One day, as I was riding back to camp, a fellow rode out in front of me with a revolver in his hand; he held it close to my nose telling me to throw up my hands. I was wearing the grizzly skin for *a cloak and had concealed my right arm in it. I threw up my left arm telling him I had but one. 'That so,' said he, lowering his pistol. 'Wal, I want yer hoss, savvy to the racket?' 'Yes,' I said, 'heap good savvy,' and like lightning I put my pistol between his eyes, and told him to drop his pistol and jump off his horse which he did. I caught his horse with my left hand, keeping the road agent covered with my pistol in my right and, digging spurs into my horse, was gone followed by half a dozen bullets from the road agent's pistol. Thus I got a good horse and saddle.*

Years later Owen Roscomyl wrote about his adventures in a number of magazines. Here he recounts how he came across a missionary:

The winter before, we had been clearing the range of buffalo to make room for the cattle we had brought up from the south over the old Texas Trail. To clear the range was no easy job. Cartridges were served out to us, and we were paid wages to hunt the buffalo – but not to kill them. The hundreds we could kill would never shift the myriad of buffalo crowding the plain. Our work was to ride into the masses of buffalo and wound, not kill, some of the leaders of each herd, so that they would fly from the range where they got hurt, leading the rest with them and so leaving the range clear for the cattle.

One evening the missionary rode in from nowhere, and drew rein in front of the smoke-fire, round which we were lying to escape the mosquitoes. He was certainly not a Cardi, or nobody could ever have sold him such a horse, which was the sort of horse that only a tenderfoot or an Indian would dream of riding. It was in fact an Indian cayuse, which had been given him over on the river, twenty miles across the Divide.

I heard the foreman say to him with a gesture in my direction, 'This is our Britisher'. I guessed that the guest had himself volunteered the information that he was from the Old Country, but I answered 'I'm a Welshman!' And straightway his voice came, grave as his grey eyes,

'Cymro?'

'Cymro o waed coch cyfan (a full-blooded Welshman),*' I answered, stepping across to shake hands with him. The foreman escorted the guest to supper while all the rest stayed at the fire. Arizona Joe said softly to me, 'He's a missionary!' My heart sank. That the first Welshman I had met in the west should be, not a man, but a missionary.*

'Oh, he's not an Injun missionary. He's come to mission us,' added Arizona. 'It's that affair on Blind Man's Creek. The papers down east got hold of something about it, and made so many sermons about it that he's come out to settle amongst us and build a church.' That affair on Blind Man's Creek was a bit of a shooting match, winding up with a bit of a necktie party – that is to say a shooting affray ending up with the hanging of certain one or two of the survivors, and would have attracted little extra notice had it not happened so close to the railway that the passengers on the passing mail train had seen some of it, and imagined more.

Next morning we were starting for a twenty days' little round up, and so we had to part with our guest. When we came back we learnt that the missionary had settled on the stream, midway between us and the O Bar outfit and was building a log cabin for himself, right in the trail of Indians raiding south. The chance of telling Rees, for that was his name, fell to me. I had gone to hunt some strayed horses, an evening found me so near his cabin with them, that I rode to his fire and accepted his grave invitation to dismount. I spent the night with him, talking of Wales. In the morning I gladly stayed to help him to get heavy roof logs into position, I even begged him to shift his cabin to another spot, three-hundred yards further down and three-hundred yards from the nearest bush, tree or cover of any kind that could harbour a lurking Indian or outlaw. I urged him to do it, offering to stay and help him through with the work. But he would not. 'The Indians that pass here are not looking for white men,' he said. 'They are passing to raid other Indians.' All I could do was to take the axe and, in spite of his smiling remonstrances, cut four little rifle loop-holes, one on each face of the cabin, close to the ground, so that a man lying down could fire through them. I also cut them in such unorthodox places that the defender of the cabin could get at least one shot through it before it could be detected. At parting, I left him my Winchester. He shook his head at that too, even when I told him he would need it to shoot game for his living. Nevertheless, I left it with him and fifty cartridges to boot. 'Don't forget now,' I called back over my shoulder, 'shut that wooden window every night. Never go out in the morning till you've looked all around those loop-holes. Never go straight to your cabin on coming home, but circle all round it well out, and look for tracks. And if they do jump you, then open that window and throw a bundle of blazing grass into that thicket there. That'll both burn out any beggar in the bush and let us know what's happening.'

It was at sun-up four or five days afterwards that the night-herder, driving in the horses to camp in the morning, said, quite casually, 'There's a big smoke up the creek. The missionary must ha' set the prairie a-fire.' I got up, lassoed a horse and saddled it and we all galloped towards the smoke. It was over when we got there. Two Indians lay dead close to the cabin loopholes, and we found another afterwards in the brush. But when we had ridden down the other four Indians and ended them, at the cost of one killed and two wounded to ourselves, we found the gallant missionary still

*breathing inside. He managed to shake his head at me. 'It was
wrong. I ought to have been ready to die, but there was the rifle
you'd left and the loop-holes, and... I'm a Welshman... and... I got
angry when they shot at the house and woke me. And...' The rest
was a prayer to Christ to receive him, for he felt death on him.
Three breaths more and the missionary was gone. We took him to
the railway and buried him in a Christian graveyard. We later
found out that the Indians had attacked him because the horse he
had belonged to them. Someone had killed one of them for the horse,
and they had seen it tied up near the missionary's door.*

Miss Lucy Bird and the rancher from Llanberis

One of the first in the West to keep visitors on his ranch was
Griffith Evans from Llanberis. In 1867, he bought Estes Park ranch
which lies north-west of Denver, and although Evans was very fond
of whisky the business became very successful. Four years after
starting he had ten guests staying there. In 1873, Miss Isabella Lucy
Bird came to stay. She would ride her horse like a man with her
skirt stuffed into her bloomers! They both became very friendly and
according to Miss Bird, she liked Griff Evans on sight, despite the
smell of whisky from his bushy beard. Griff would take her riding in
the hills and Miss Bird would 'deal with Griff's hangovers and
herded his cattle at such times'.

She reserved her love however for the handsome Irishman,
Mountain Jim Nugent, another one fond of his whisky. Miss Bird
left Estes Park and went to stay for some months with the Irishman
before returning to the east. But things were not too good between
the Welshman and the Irishman. In June 1874, Griff Evans shot
and killed Nugent. Evans pleaded not guilty and was acquitted, his
plea being one of self-defence. It wasn't Miss Lucy Bird that had led
to the killing, but Nugent's designs on Evans' daughter Jinnie!

4. On the railroad

Jack Farmer – Railroad Pioneer

Not everyone went to the Wild West to become outlaws, lawmen, cowboys or ranchers. Many went there to bring 'civilisation' to the area, men like Jack Farmer of Montgomeryshire who left Wales for America in 1886 to work on constructing the railways running from east to west. Farmer was one of seventy surveyors laying tracks through the Rockies in Montana, and in particular through the Macdonald Gap that was over seven thousand feet above sea level. They had to lay ten miles of track everyday through wild country and even wilder weather, weather that often added rheumatism to the men's suffering. Farmer was one of those that suffered and in order to relieve his pain he took a short break in Sulphur Springs. A very bad place, according to Farmer, with many women trying to persuade men to fall by the wayside! But, according to Farmer, he resisted temptation.

Before leaving Sulphur Springs, to stop the rheumatism returning, Farmer went for the Whisky Cure and bought a cask of

Jack Farmer in a photograph he sent home to his family

Jack Farmer in the railway company camp

Kentucky Bourbon to take back with him to camp.

In the beginning the cask was very heavy and he struggled to carry it to his tent, but as time went by the cask became much easier to carry and the rheumatism had disappeared!

But it wasn't just rheumatism and bad women that were a danger to the railwaymen. The Indians did not want the 'iron horse' crossing their lands, frightening the buffalo and bringing more whites into their territories. They would often attack the track-laying gangs and for men like Farmer it was dangerous work as they had to travel ahead of everyone else. They would carry guns with them to defend themselves and armed men were hired to guard the camps, men like Buffalo Bill and Wild Bill Hickock who would also shoot buffalo to feed the railwaymen.

5. The Welsh and the Indians

Indians (or Amerindians to use the proper term) most probably reached North America about 20,000 years ago, crossing from Asia to Alaska across the Bering Straits. When the white men first reached North America there were probably about a million Indians in about three hundred tribes and about the same number of languages there. Amongst the tribes in the West were the Apache, Arapaho, Bannock, Blackfoot, Cayuse, Cherokee, Cheyenne, Chinook, Comanche, Crow, Hopi, Kiowa, Mandan (who, some say, were descended from Madog and his men, the Welsh Prince who arrived in America during the 11th century), Navaho, Nez Percé, Osage, Paiute, Pawnee, Shoshone, Sioux, Ute and the Zuni.

Some were nomadic hunting tribes, others were settled in villages and grew crops. Their houses varied enormously – from the *tepee* which we usually associate with the Plains Indians to the pueblo villages of the south-west tribes. The various tribes would trade with each other, and since the Indians had not invented the wheel they used sledges dragged by dogs or canoes to carry loads. But once the Spaniards arrived in North America, the Indians caught some of their horses and became excellent horsemen.

To the Indians, war was a game and it was very rarely that they would completely defeat their enemies. Because of this, the fighting between the natives and the early whites was not intense. It was only when they started losing their lands and hunting grounds that the Indians started seriously to fight the whites. Indians would not usually fight at night as they believed that if they were killed in battle, their spirits could not find their way to heaven.

As the whites moved West, the Indians were moved from their lands which led to fierce battles in many instances, with the Welsh along with other nationalities caught up in the fighting. Many were killed, but others were fortunate to escape.

This is how the Reverend William Davies Evans describes the American Indians in his book *Dros Gyfanfor a Chyfandir* (Over Ocean and Continent):

> *They came with wild animals' skins to be sold or bartered for the white man's goods. The squaws tried to dress in the fashion of the white women, but much untidier. They had moccasins on their feet and with long, coarse, straight hair. One could see from afar that they were Indians from their motion. They walked quickly, one after the other. They stopped suddenly when stopping, and stood as straight as poles. They turned their faces to look over their shoulders. They then walked back quickly, as if they had discovered something that they needed to go to. When they came to the wall of a house, they stooped and looked around the corner, as they did when hiding behind a tree or rock spying for an enemy or prey. They did not sit, they squatted until their knees were as high as their mouths. They had large red faces, thoughtful looks, serious and determined.*

W R Jones and his first encounter with Indians

During the mid nineteenth century, many Welsh men and women emigrated to Minnesota, amongst them was W R Jones and his family from Aberffraw, Anglesey. After reaching the area in 1858, the family settled in Judson. Later that year, Jones returned with a wagon and a team of oxen to Rochester to fetch the rest of his belongings. It was a three-day journey and at the end of the first day he found good grazing land for the oxen and decided to stay the night there.

Jones was about to put his blankets down for the night when seven or eight Indians on horseback came towards him. They stopped their horses a few yards away, each one having a bow,

William R Jones' house in Judson

arrows and a knife. Some of them went to the wagon, but it was empty. They saw Jones' blankets on the ground and they started rummaging amongst them. Jones let them be as he didn't want to antagonise them, but there was nothing they wanted there, so that they started shouting, "Money, money!" Jones shook his head, as he had none on him. Then the Indians shouted, "Bacco, bacco!" But Jones' English was as scarce as the Indians' and all he could say was, "No bacco! No bacco!" With their whoops echoing in the valley, the Indians jumped onto their mounts and disappeared, much to the relief of the Welshman.

But there was worse to come. Judson was located in Butternut Valley, an area known today as Cambria and W R Jones lived there when many were killed during the Butternut Valley Massacre. Although the Indians did not attack Judson, many refugees – Welsh, German and English – came to the village and Jones and his family looked after some of them. This is the only time that Indians attacked any Welsh settlements.

The Butternut Valley Massacre

In 1853 many of the Sioux tribes had to sign a treaty with the United States government and they were restricted to two reservations at the head of the Minnesota river, about twenty miles from where a number of Welsh men and women had settled and about fifteen miles from Fort Ridgeley which guarded the area. Once a year the tribes would receive money and goods as part of the treaty, but usually these payments were late and much less than what had been agreed because the agents and merchants had taken their cut. By 1862 the Indians had had enough; more whites were coming to the area and the wild animals on which they relied on for food were becoming scarcer. Therefore, the Indians under the leadership of Little Crow decided to try and get rid of all the whites who lived to the west of the Mississippi.

They first attacked Fort Ridgeley and if it was not for the perseverance of a young Welshman called Sergeant Jones they would have overrun the fort. There were only eighty soldiers in the fort as the rest had gone east to fight in the Civil War; also many of the local men had enlisted to go and fight in the northern army. When the Indians came to the fort, Sergeant Jones was the only one who thought that they would attack and he insisted that everyone should stay at his post through the afternoon and night with their guns ready. But the following morning, the Indians left as they saw that the soldiers were ready for them.

But they didn't return to the reservation. They attacked the settlement of Lower Agency, killing everyone and destroying all the properties. They then attacked the outlying farms and refugees began to arrive in the town of New Ulm which was not very far from Cambria where the Welsh had settled. The inhabitants decided to form a militia to guard the area and many Welshmen volunteered to join. William J Jones and others from Judson

A map of the Welsh territories in Minnesota

travelled to New Ulm to defend the town from any attacks. Wagons and trees were put across the streets of New Ulm to stop the Indians. Then, at four o'clock in the afternoon, Little Crow and his Indians attacked and burnt many of the houses on the outskirts of the town.

News of the Indian attacks reached the town of South Bend and a militia was raised of about eighty men – over half of them Welshmen – to help the inhabitants of New Ulm. On their way there, they picked up more men from Judson. In the meantime, the Welsh in Cambria had heard the bad news and had congregated in a number of houses for safety. But the following morning, they decided to leave the area for the protection of South Bend and Mankato.

By this time, nearly five hundred men had reached New Ulm, none of them professional soldiers. Very few had modern rifles, some had shotguns, others only had scythes and pitchforks. For three days, they waited for the Indians to attack, but nothing happened, and many became worried about their families who had been left unprotected. About eighty, therefore, decided to leave for home.

The following morning the Indians attacked New Ulm, fighting from house to house, pushing the whites back. Little Crow had placed his men at the head of each street and they would shoot at anyone trying to cross. But the whites had to cross, with messages and ammunition. Many had been killed attempting this and they were having trouble finding volunteers for the job. Then, Thomas Davies volunteered and he ran backwards and forwards all day, avoiding the bullets. In the meantime, the South Bend militia were on their way back to New Ulm, with Welshmen William Jones and David and John Davies amongst them. When they got near the town, they saw smoke rising and feared the worst. They, therefore, decided to return to South Bend with the bad news that all New Ulm's inhabitants had been killed and the town burnt to the ground.

Some of the Welshmen had returned to Cambria to check their stock and they also had seen the smoke. They advised everyone to leave the farms and seek the comparative safety of South Bend and Mankato. In South Bend, hundreds of women and children had arrived and were staying in Evans and Price's mill whilst their menfolk were preparing to defend the town. Once again, they had very few modern weapons, and they spent an anxious night with the fires of New Ulm illuminating the sky. Many of the women were worried about their men, who had gone to protect New Ulm.

By this time, the bad news had reached Governor Ramsey in St Paul where many soldiers were preparing to leave to fight in the Civil War. He ordered a company, many of them Welshmen, to return west to protect the whites from the Indians and about a hundred and twenty went to New Ulm. But when they arrived, the Indians had decided that they weren't likely to defeat the inhabitants and they had left. Twenty nine whites had been killed and over fifty wounded in the town itself whilst there were many more casualties in the outlying districts. Everyone was ordered to leave New Ulm in case the Indians returned. Since so many had already arrived in South Bend they had to travel onwards to Mankato, and in order to feed everyone there John and David Evans and Thomas Jones killed two large oxen whilst Elizabeth Davies baked bread for the refugees.

One day, a man arrived in South Bend in a bad way. He had been shot seven times and had travelled over eighty miles in three days through territories held by the Indians. He had come to fetch help for women and children who had been left on their own in the middle of the Sioux. It was decided to send fourteen men, including Welshmen Lewis Jones, David Davies and William Williams, under the leadership of Lieutenant Roberts to look for the women and children. They could not send more as they wanted them to protect the town. They eventually reached them, all hiding in one house. They were put in a wagon and everyone returned to South Bend by a different route in case the Indians were waiting for them.

The same day, David Davis and his sons were out harvesting in their fields in the Cambria area. Towards the end of the day, one of the sons, Eben, went to keep the horses but suddenly an Indian jumped out of the long grass. The Welshmen ran for the trees but not before Eben had been shot in the wrist.

Everyone heard of the incident and gathered in James Morgan's house for protection and to plan to protect the area. But luckily, a troop of soldiers arrived and set up camp for a few days near Horeb Chapel. Even so, about thirty Welsh men, women and children would gather in James Morgan's house every night. One morning, after the soldiers had left, everyone were awakened by the dogs barking and James Morgan went to the door where he saw someone dressed as a white man. But on looking carefully, he saw that it was an Indian. He shouted for Lewis Lewis to come to the doorway. Lewis raised his hand to shelter his eyes from the strong sun, but suddenly there was a shot and a bullet went through Lewis's hand and into his head. Although he was badly wounded, his hand had saved his life. Inside the house, James Edwards went for his gun but a bullet came through one of the windows and struck him in his neck. He fell to the floor, dead with his blood flowing onto the cabin floor. Everyone rushed for their guns and started firing through the windows. The fierce battle lasted for some

Lieutenant John Roberts who led the men who went to find the women who had been left amongst the Indians

hours; no more Welshmen were hit although many of the Indians were shot and they eventually disappeared into the woods.

John and Henry Davies then decided to go and look for the soldiers and told everyone to stay in the house. But, as there was no sign of the Indians, they decided to leave and they ran towards a small stream which they followed. But a mile or so after leaving the house, they saw some Sioux warriors coming in their direction and they jumped into some bushes to hide with the Indians passing within a few feet of them.

In the meantime, to the west, David Davies had asked his son to go and fetch the cattle from the corn but some Indians saw him and fired at him, hitting in the back with the bullet going through his heart. Davies saw his son being shot, so he got the rest of the family together and fled down the valley.

Richard Wigley, William Roberts and John Jones had left the area near Horeb Chapel with a threshing machine but after a few miles had come across the people from James Morgan's house coming towards them. They were warned that there were Indians in the area, but they decided to proceed with their journey as they had

Horeb Chapel where the soldiers camped with James Morgan's house which the Indians attacked on 10 September 1862

work to do in fields owned by two men called Mohr and Trask. They had barely started working when they saw Indians coming towards them. Mohr and Trask started firing at the Indians, but one was shot in his forehead and the other in his hand. The Welshmen had no weapons on them, so they decided to run into a sugarcane field to hide and the Indians spent some time looking for them. They came nearer and nearer, but suddenly there came the sound of horses approaching. A troop of soldiers were on their way and the Indians fled, but not before stealing one of the horses from the threshing machine.

The hanging of 36 Sioux Indians in Mankato, 26 December 1862. Three hundred Indians were imprisoned in the buildings in the background during the winter of 1862-3

A few days later, the Sioux came across Robert Jones and John Shaw building a hayrick. When they saw Indians approaching, they decided to make a run for it. Shaw escaped but that was the last time that anyone saw Jones alive. His son, Evan, had seen the Indians shooting at his father and had gone into a ditch to hide. Such was his fear of the Indians, that he stayed there for ten days until some soldiers found him. The following spring, David Davies was clearing land when he came across Robert Jones' bones lying in the grass where he had been killed by the Indians.

The fighting between the Indians and the whites lasted for two

months but more and more soldiers came to the area. In September, twenty-two Welshmen came together to build a fort to defend the area. A few days later there was a huge battle between Little Crow and eight hundred of his followers and 1,500 soldiers under the command of a Colonel Sibley. Thirty Indians were killed, with four soldiers dead and within a few weeks two thousand Sioux warriors surrendered with the rest fleeing to Dakota where they periodically continued to attack the whites.

During the two months of fighting, a thousand whites were killed with many more injured. Three hundred Indians were sentenced to death; most were pardoned by President Abraham Lincoln with only thirty-six being hanged. The rest were imprisoned.

The Miners and the Indians

In 1851, **Edward R Williams** and others travelled on a steamer from San Francisco to northern California as they had heard that gold had been found in the area. After landing, they had to walk through vast forests, inhabited by Indians who were generally quite friendly with the miners and bartered with them. But, when Williams and the others were walking along a narrow path through the forest, they were surrounded by Indians. There was no place to escape so they all pulled out their guns and aimed them at the Indians. The warriors, seeing that they had no chance against the armed miners, gave one deafening whoop and disappeared into the trees. But two of the miners were way behind the others, leading pack mules, and they had no chance against the Indians. The miners heard shots and saw the mules running towards them. They decided that there was not much that could be done for the two miners, so they proceeded on their journey to try and get out of the forest as soon as possible.

Later that day, they had to stop to shelter from a snowstorm. They had reached a large rock and they managed to put up a tent in the lee to form a shelter from the cold wind. Suddenly, they saw some Indians coming towards them, and they took out their guns and started firing at them. The Indians fired back from amongst the trees, but left after a quarter of an hour, dragging their wounded with them. When the snowstorm passed, the miners continued with their journey and eventually got out of the forest some days later and reached the goldfields.

Another Welshman who came across the Indians whilst looking for gold was **Richard D Owens**. In a letter to his uncle dated 21 February 1876 from Custer City, Dakota, Owens tells of his journey to the Black Hills to look for gold.

I've been travelling for sixteen days. I left Colorado on 1 February, taking the train as far as Cheyenne, Wyoming Territory. I stayed the night in Cheyenne and left the following morning. There were two wagonloads of us starting out, comprising ten people. As we went on, we met a few wagons coming from other places and after arriving at Fort Laramie, ninety-three miles from Cheyenne, there were nine wagons containing thirty-nine men, besides their wives and children. Each of us was armed to meet the Indians but we got through without trouble. The white men are worse than the Indians. Two horses were stolen one night from a man travelling with us and after that we chose men from the band to watch over our things and to stand guard at night in case the Indians attacked us from the rear. There were seven men on guard each night, every four hours. But I do not think the Indians will trouble us until the weather gets warmer.

Many people are coming here and twelve to fifteen reach Custer

City every day. Undoubtedly, there is gold here, but whether there is
enough for a man to make a living is another matter. The talk here
at the moment is about the Big Horn and everyone saying that the
best mines are there but the snow is deep now and the Indians
dangerous. The latest news I heard from there was that the Indians
had killed two men and were stealing as many horses as they could.
I heard also that many soldiers had gone there and were stopping
men from emigrating there.

Another letter, this time from **Thomas Davies** who was in Silver
Cliff, Custer County, Colorado, says that the government was
driving the Indians from their lands and that the Welsh were
welcome to come over and look for gold:

A law has been passed for the Utes Indians to leave their reservation
so that whites can go in to find minerals and to farm the land.
There is good agricultural land in the reservation, the best in the
state and wonderful minerals there too. What a place for a Welsh
settlement, boys! Come out here when the Indians leave! We, the
Welsh in Colorado, have chosen two men to go to the reservation to
choose the best land for a new Welsh settlement. John M Jones from
Ffestiniog went to the reservation last spring and says that it is
excellent for miners, for prospectors, and farmers. He has eaten with
the Utes and finds nothing horrible in them. Don't be afraid of the
Indians, boys! The government has prepared a place for them in
Utah and New Mexico.

Daniel Williams and the Wagon Train

We've already heard of Daniel Williams of Penmaen,
Monmouthshire, in the goldfields of Montana. On the way there,
he called at Rock Island, Illinois, and then travelled through

Kearney, Fort Laramie and Sweetwater, with twenty other men and one woman in a train of nine wagons. But on the way there, they were fortunate not to be killed by Indians and they had to be rescued by the army. This is part of a talk Williams gave to the Montana Pioneers in Butte, Montana, in 1895 or 1896:

We had camped one night on the banks of Antelope Creek, where red clover was growing abundantly and where the fishing and hunting was excellent. We had seen no signs of Indians and being anxious to avail ourselves of the hunting and fishing, we did not corral our wagons as was our usual custom but left them in a line where each one had come to a halt.

About eleven o'clock that night we were startled by an Indian war-cry and several rifle shots. The leader of the wagon train having directed me to choose a companion and go out to reconnoitre, I chose John Perkins, not only because he was a brave man, but because he had a gun that was a small cannon in its way and would take twice as large a charge of slugs as a common shotgun. We did not have occasion to shoot at the Indians, however, but discovered there was a war party of about forty of them.

During our absence our party corralled the wagons and secured the stock. The Indians made no further attack on us during the night, but when we started on the morning we could catch glimpse of them in the hills about, flanking us in on every side. What made the situation more desperate was that four miles further on the road entered a narrow canyon, where we would be almost at their mercy. Fully expecting that our end was near, those of the party who could be spared from active duty were writing notes to absent friends and dropping them in the sage brush by the roadside.

Suddenly one of the men on the watch shouted that he saw a soldier, then more appeared, and we soon met General Connor with

*companies of cavalry and infantry from Fort Bridges. He told us
that they had doubtless saved us from complete massacre as there
were a thousand hostile Snake warriors in the immediate vicinity.
Our escape during the night had been due to the fact that the
Indians were short of ammunition, and knowing the approach of
General Connor, they had saved their powder and balls for the
soldiers instead of wasting them on tenderfoot emigrants.*

But not all the Welsh wanted to fight the Indians. Some fell in
love and married Indian women.

Robert Big Eyes and Chief Blue Horse's Grand-daughter

One of these was Robert Owen Pugh of Dolgellau who married the
grand-daughter of Chief Blue Horse of the Oglala Sioux.
Robert Pugh was sixteen years old when he sailed from Liverpool to
New York in 1863, and then travelled to Wyoming where he got
work on a ranch. One day, out on the range on his own, he came
across a band of Shoshone. He rushed to a nearby cabin which the
men used, but the Indians surrounded it and started firing. Pugh
knew he wouldn't be able to survive long against the Shoshone.
Then he had an idea. The men had left their rifles in the cabin and
in order to give the impression that there was more than one with
him, Pugh poked each rifle out of the windows and
ran around the cabin firing each gun. Then he
started shouting, using different voices. After
about twenty minutes, the Indians thinking
that there were many in the cabin, gave up
and left, and Pugh jumped on his horse and

Robert Owen Pugh

74

galloped to the safety of the ranch.

A few months later, he moved further west, eventually reaching the Black Hills of Dakota. At first, he found work driving wagons and stagecoaches between Cheyenne and Deadwood, but later on he moved onto the Oglala reservation to keep a store and became a clerk to the local Indian agent. There, in Pine Ridge, Dakota, in 1888, he married Jenny Blue Horse (Robinson), grand-daughter of Chief Blue Horse. She had been given the surname Robinson as she had been born in Fort Robinson, Dakota.

Jennie Blue Horse

Her grandfather, Chief Blue Horse, had taken part in the Battle of the Little Big Horn where Custer and the 7th Cavalry were killed. Pugh came to know many of the chiefs of the period, men such as Crazy Horse, Spotted Tail and Man Afraid of His Horse, and the Indians' name for Pugh was *Istachtonka* or Big Eyes.

The couple had two children and the family was in the area during the Wounded Knee Massacre when hundreds of Indians were killed. Because of the troubles, Pugh moved his family to a safer area. Sitting Bull had returned to the reservation from Canada where he had fled after the Battle of the Little Big Horn but he was shot dead on 15 December 1890 by two Indian policemen who were trying to arrest him. Fearing more trouble, the Sioux decided to leave the reservation and travelled towards the Cheyenne River. This frightened the army and 3,000 soldiers were ordered into the area. By 29 December, 500 soldiers had surrounded 350 Indians camping in Wounded Knee Creek. The soldiers fired their cannon into the camp and then shot at the Indians with their rifles. Many were killed instantly but some managed to escape with the soldiers pursuing them. Each one was eventually caught and shot or beaten to death.

Robert and Jennie's children

After things quietened down on the reservation, Pugh and his family returned, but after a few years he sold his store and took over the post office. He became a man respected by the Indians, and in 1895 Pugh was a member of the First Council which held negotiations with the American Government about selling land in the Black Hills. There are many references to Robert O Pugh in the history books and a street in Martin was named after him.

The Indians were very unhappy with how they were treated by the government and its agents. Some of them, especially Chief Red Cloud, refused to send his children to schools set up by the whites. But the Indians, also, did not receive what was due to them under the treaty signed in 1876 when the Oglala Sioux ceded their lands to the whites and moved onto the reservations. Part of the deal was that the Sioux were to receive food, clothing and farming implements, but the local Indian agent had employed a number of dubious characters and they were stealing and selling what was due to the Indians. Red Cloud and other chiefs went to Washington with their grievances, and the result was that the Holman Committee was set up in 1884 to look at the situation and one who gave evidence to the committee was R O Pugh.

In 1906, Judge E S Risker who had worked for the Indian Affairs Bureau in Washington for ten years questioned Pugh who gave him a description of the pitiful circumstances that the Indians lived in – short of food and materials, and even what they received was arriving late. Pugh described the Indians as noble people. Here is part of his testimony to Judge Risker:

> *I came amongst them 36 years ago with the usual impressions of the white man that they were more akin to animals than men; but I have changed my mind since then, and of the opinion that they should be treated like men. The government does not play fair with them; its policies towards them are wrong; they are sent from place to place contrary to any justice and they are considered as naughty children.*

But Pugh's family was not of the same opinion as him and they were not happy that he had married an Indian. When his sister Mary heard what his situation was, she went all the way to South Dakota to try and persuade him to come home! Before then, she had written many letters to Pugh describing the Indians as uncivilised savages. Jenny Blue Horse saw these letters and told the rest of the tribe what Big Eyes's sister thought of them, and when Mary arrived in Pine Ridge she was not welcome. She had to stay in an old cabin on the edge of the village, with her brother having to visit her after dark so that the Indians would not see him! But Mary failed to persuade him to return to Wales and Robert Owen Pugh stayed amongst the Oglala Sioux and died there in 1922 and was buried in Hot Springs. Some Welshmen, and indeed many of the whites who moved West, had an ambivalent attitude towards the Indians. They both admired them and fought with them. One such man was Old Solitaire.

Wild Bill Williams – Indian Scout and Adventurer

Bill Williams was born in Tennessee, his family having emigrated there from Denbighshire. He was brought up amongst the Osage Indians and learnt many of their skills and traditions. He also learnt to speak their language. Young Williams was an impressive-looking man – over six feet tall, with red hair and freckles. His father was an itinerant Baptist preacher, also his brother Lewis and two uncles, and it was no surprise that Williams followed in their footsteps. Williams became a missionary amongst the Indians in Missouri for many years, but he was not successful and turned to alcohol in his desperation.

When he was 26 years old, he married a member of the Osage tribe, and although he spent much time in the mountains as hunter, trapper and guide, they had two red-haired daughters. As he could, by now, speak many Indian languages and was a sharpshooter, he was employed many a time by the US Army as a scout. He spent many years travelling backwards and forwards from Missouri to the Rocky Mountains. He was an expert on mountain life and was known as 'king of the mountains', and as he spent so much time alone he also became known as Old Solitaire.

He moved to Santa Fé, New Mexico, when he was 38 years old where he spent much of his time drinking and gambling in the

Robert Owen Pugh with his rifle in the Post Office, in the early 1900s

numerous saloons. One time, he won a considerable amount of money and decided to open a small store in Taos. But he wasn't cut out to be a storekeeper, and within a short period he decided to share out the stock amongst the Indians and Mexicans!

In the summer of 1832, Williams was a part of a band of hunters under the command of Captain Bonneville which travelled to the Uintah Mountains on the border of Colorado, Wyoming and Utah. To help out with various chores, Williams got hold of twelve female members of the Bannack tribe, but this was not very successful as eight of the hunters were stabbed to death fighting over the women! Although Williams had been brought up amongst the Indians, and reputedly had married two of them, he had very little respect for them. In 1833, he was part of a band of men that reached California and there they spent their time stealing women and hides from the Shoshone. Earlier, they had killed about two dozen members of the Paiute tribe when trying to steal their squaws. But it was not only from the Indians that Williams and his band stole from. Later that year, with Joe Meek and Peg Leg Smith, he spent time stealing horses from the Spanish-owned ranches in the area. Sometimes they stole as many as three thousand horses, drove them east and either sold them to the US Army at Bent's Fort or to the Apaches!

About 1842, Williams and his old friend, the famous hunter and scout Kit Carson, went back east and Williams saw his daughters for the first time in many years. But he soon returned to the life he had got used to. He led many an expedition over the Rockies, his last with General John C Fremont over to California. At the end of that journey, Williams and a few men returned to the mountains to look for equipment that they had left there. One morning towards the end of March 1850, when they were in the territory of the Utes, Williams got up early and decided to go scouting on his own. But he didn't return, and the rest of the band went looking for him. The following morning they found him, lying face down with Ute arrows in his back. Although Williams had killed hundreds of Indians in his day, he was on good terms with the Utes and the belief is that they had killed him by mistake. When the Indians found out who they had killed, they gave him a burial ceremony worthy of a chief. Williams' exploits are still commemorated in the West; in Arizona there is a town called Williams, a Bill Williams Mountain and a Bill Williams River.

6. In the Army

There were two occurrences that led to thousands of white people travelling west; America victorious in the war against Mexico in 1849 gaining vast tracts of land in the south-west and the discovery of gold in Sutter's Creek, California, later in the same year. Thousands of hunters, trappers, farmers and prospectors travelled westwards across the wide plains and over the high mountains, battling not only the inhospitable terrain but also the extreme weather. At first the Native Americans accepted them, but as they realised that the white man was stealing their land and killing the wildlife on which they depended to live on, the situation soon changed and they began attacking the whites. The army was sent west to guard the whites and forts were built in the area to where the whites could retreat in the event of attacks.

At first, the army sent infantry and artillery companies, but the authorities in Washington soon realised that they needed an army that could move fast against an enemy, who mainly fought a guerrilla war. A cavalry unit was much more expensive to maintain; not only had they to buy horses but they also had to feed them; army horses needed grain and could not survive on the wild grasses of the prairie as could the Indian ponies.

It took quite a few years before the cavalry arrived in the West, but in those early years there were not many attacks on the whites. But in 1855 a band of Sioux attacked a stagecoach and then shot a ferry operator on the River Platte. These modes of transport were important in opening up the West and therefore a company of the 2nd Dragoons was sent to arrest the Indians, but they were all killed. Then cavalry was sent to the area, and on 2 September 1855 they engaged the Sioux and killed 85 of them with the loss of four soldiers. The cavalry had proved its worth and from then onwards, cavalry companies were the main units in the West.

From then onwards there were continuous skirmishes between the Indians and the army, often due to white men breaking treaties signed with the Indians, usually by moving onto land allocated to the Indians to look for gold or other metals or for farming land. Many Indians were killed and the rest moved onto reservations where conditions were poor with no wildlife for hunting and many miles from their ancestral grounds. On 15 January 1891, a band of Sioux surrendered to the army in North Dakota which signalled the end of the fighting. Six days later, the 6th, 7th and 9th Cavalry and the 1st Infantry congregated in the Pine Ridge Agency for the last time before they were disbanded or moved back east. The wars with the Plains Indians were over.

John Davies – recipient of the Indian Medal

Many Welshmen joined the US Army, with many of them sent west to fight the Indians. One of these was John Davies who was seven years old when he left south Wales in 1875. The family settled in Ohio where the father worked as a miner, but Davies did not follow in his footsteps and in 1887 he joined the army. He was in an artillery battalion and was sent west to protect the whites from Indian attacks. Although it is the cavalry we usually see in films as they were in the majority, there were also many foot soldiers fighting in the west. These soldiers would march from one fort to another, following the heavy guns being pulled by horses. John Davies took part in many skirmishes with the Indians and he was awarded the Indian Medal for his services.

But his army career ended in disgrace. He was court-martialled for refusing to obey an officer – he refused to eat pork which he thought had not been properly cooked – and incited others to do the same. Although he was later acquitted, he was discharged from the service. But four years later, he changed his name to Joe Orfant (no-one in the family knows where this name came from) and joined the marines, seeing service in Cuba and the Philippines.

Gregory Mahoney and the 4th Cavalry

Another Welshman who joined the US Army was Gregory Mahoney of West Street, Pontypool. Mahoney travelled west with the 4th Cavalry and was involved in many battles with Indians. His company at one time had been ordered to look for a band of Comanche which had been attacking wagon trains travelling across the plains. But the Indians found the cavalry first and attacked them. There was nowhere to hide on the flat prairie and the Indians attacked them mercilessly. The captain decided that they would attack the Comanche coming from an eastern direction, hoping that they would be able to break through and make a dash for a nearby fort which was some miles away. The soldiers attacked, each one with his sabre in his hand, into the midst of the Indians. Many of the cavalrymen were cut down by the bullets and arrows of the Indians, leaving many of them dead. Mahoney, having lost his horse and sabre, used his revolver, and fought hand to hand with the Comanche warriors.

With the end in sight for the cavalrymen, suddenly, in the distance, they could hear a bugle calling. Another troop of the 4th Cavalry was on its way to rescue them. The Comanches jumped on their horses and galloped back into the hills. After burying the dead, the cavalrymen returned to the safety of the fort. Later, in 1875, Gregory Mahoney received the Congressional Medal of Honour for his bravery.

Sol Rees – Army Scout

Solomon Rees also fought the Indians with the US Army, but as a scout rather than a regular soldier. He was born in Delaware county, Indiana, in 1847; his father's family from south-west Wales and his mother's family from Anglesey. After fighting on the Union side during the American Civil War, he married a girl with both Indian and Welsh blood in her, and they then lived on a reservation in east Kansas. But he could not settle down, and took to the plains hunting buffalo for the railroads. When the Cheyenne were driven onto reservations in Oklahoma, Sol Rees was employed by the 4th Cavalry to accompany them. It was during this time that he came to know the famous Indian fighter Kit Carson. He was paid five dollars a day as this official document in the possession of the Rees family shows:

```
Office Acting Asst. Quartermaster, USA
Fort Wallace, Kansas, Nov. 4, 1878

Sol Rees, Citizen Scout, has this day presented to
me a certificate, given him by Major Mock, Fourth
US Cavalry, for thirty-nine days' service as scout
and guide, at $5 per day, amounting to one hundred
and ninety-five dollars. This certificate I have
forwarded to Department Headquarters, asking
authority and funds to pay Rees's claim. On a
favourable reply and funds being furnished, I will
pay the claim.

George M Love
1st Lieut. 16th Inf., Acting Asst. Q. M.
```

Chief of the Cheyenne was Dull Knife. The Indians did not like their new lands near Fort Reno so in 1878 they decided to leave with the US Army in hot pursuit. Sol Rees was in Texas at the time and a runner was sent to ask him to return to work for the army. This he did and returned to Kansas where he came across many whites who had been attacked by the Cheyenne. He formed a posse after some difficulty and went in pursuit of the Indians. They came across a band of Cheyenne but no-one – apart from Rees – wanted to attack them. Rees rushed towards them, emptying his revolver in their direction, but the Indians

Sol Rees

escaped. Rees followed them and eventually came across one of them dead on the trail, with four bullets in his body. Rees scalped him.

Later, they came across a troop of 4th Cavalry who were very angry as the Cheyenne had just killed their leader, Colonel Lewis. Rees and his band joined them in pursuit of his killers. This is how Sol Rees recounted his experience to John R Cooke, author of *The Border and the Buffalo:*

We followed the trail down on the Beaver [river]; and there we got into a mess. We found where the Indians had butchered four men. They had been digging potatoes and had been hacked to pieces by the hoes they were using in their work. Evidently, this had been done by squaws and small boys, for all the moccasin-tracks indicated it. The hogpen had been opened, so that the hogs could eat the bodies.

That night we went on to the Republican River … The Indians camped about three miles above. The next morning we went there and struck their last night's camp. They had not long gone, for there were live coals from the willow-brush fires. They struck for the breaks of the North Fork of the Republican. Across the divide, and coming up on the breaks to the north, we could see the Indians, and they us, at the same time. The Indians started to run. We took the trail, which was now easily followed. Packs were dropped, worn-out ponies left on the trail, as well as many garments carried from the settlers' homes.

Sol Rees fighting an Indian (from the book The Border and The Buffalo*)*

> *Amos Chapman [another scout] and I were now riding together,*
> *when we saw a pack ahead of us that looked peculiar. I dismounted*
> *to look at it. It was a live Indian. Pulling out my six-shooter I*
> *would have killed him, but Amos said, 'Don't, Sol.' Amos was a*
> *good sign-talker, and tried to talk to him, but he was stoical and*
> *silent. I put my 45 to his ear and said: "Ame, it's signs or death.' He*
> *seemed to realise what would come, and sign-talk he did, a-plenty.*
> *He said he was tired out, and could not keep up, and his people had*
> *left him, not having time to make a travois [sledge] to take him*
> *along. When the wagons came up this played-out warrior was*
> *loaded onto one, and hauled for two days, when some of the soldiers,*
> *who loved their dead Colonel Lewis, sent him home to the 'happy*
> *hunting-grounds' by the bullet route.*

After weeks fleeing from the soldiers, the Indians were
surrounded near Fort Robinson, Nebraska, but after fierce fighting
they managed to escape towards Fort Keogh, Montana, where they
were captured. Rees got further work taking the 300 Cheyenne back
to Kansas, and although he was offered more work by the army, he
decided to return to his home in Prairie Dog in north-west Kansas.
But as Rees said, "I am of a restless disposition. So I rented out my
farm and went to New Mexico, and was gone three years."

While in Raton, he was struck by mountain fever. Kit Carson's
widow heard that he was lying unconscious somewhere in town so
she sent four strong men to look for him and carry him to her
home. She looked after him for five days and nights until he became
better, and to pay her for her kindness, Rees gave her twenty dollars
to buy soap, washtubs and boards to start a laundry business in
Raton. Rees then returned to his home in Prairie Dog, to his wife
and five children.

Sergeant William B James
and the Battle of the Little Bighorn

One who joined the 7th Cavalry and was killed with General George Custer in the Battle of the Little Bighorn or Custer's Last Stand was William Bowen James of Pencnwc Farm, Dinas, near Haverfordwest. James was born in 1849 and by 1870 he had emigrated to America and was working as a coachman in Chicago. In 1872, when he was twenty-three years old, he joined the army and by 1876 he was a sergeant in E Company 7th Cavalry based in Montana looking for Chief Sitting Bull who was on the warpath.

On Sunday morning, 25th June, Custer decided to split the 7th Cavalry into three battalions under the command of Major Reno, Captain Benteen and himself. C, E, F, I and L troops were with Custer and they aimed for one of the Indian villages which they were going to attack. Bu the Indians, comprising members of the Sioux, Cheyenne, Arapaho and Gros Ventres, had seen them coming. Three thousand Indians attacked Custer and his men and within minutes the cavalrymen dismounted and tried to form a circle to defend themselves from the Indians until the other two battalions could rescue them. But the Indians had attacked the other battalions as well. Wave after wave of Indians attacked Custer's men, and within half an hour the battle was over, with 261 soldiers lying dead on the valley floor. Amongst them were Sergeant William B James and General George Custer.

Trooper Frank Roberts and his distrust of the Indians

Many of the Welsh men and women had *hiraeth* for the old country and many returned, some permanently such as Robert Samuel Kenrick and William Davies, others just for a short period such as Frank Roberts, son of the Golden Age tavern in Pen-y-graig near Tonypandy. Roberts was a member of the 3rd United States Cavalry and Mounted Infantry for twelve years and was with them when Chief Sitting Bull of the Sioux surrendered in July 1881. Before then, he had taken part in numerous skirmishes with the Indians. According to Trooper Roberts in his letters home, he did not trust the Indians. He alleged that the Indians knew much more English than they admitted, and according to him, when the soldiers attacked them, they would shout, "Come on, you white-livered sons of bitches!"

In 1891, Roberts returned to Wales to see his family and friends, but he could not keep away from the Wild West, and when Buffalo Bill's Wild West Show came to Cardiff he was one of the show's most regular visitors. After four months home in Wales, Roberts returned to America and joined the 3rd Cavalry.

Members of the 3rd Cavalry near Fort Davis, Texas, about 1886

Buffalo Bill's Wild West Show

Another visitor to Buffalo Bill's show in Cardiff was a grocer from Cathays. During the same year as Roberts' visit to the show, a grocer from Cardiff went up to Colonel 'Buffalo' Bill Cody and asked him if he remembered him from his days in the Wild West. Cody replied that he didn't, accused him of telling lies and sent him packing. The grocer went to the nearest barbershop, shaved off his beard and trimmed his moustache and returned to the show. Cody immediately recognised him and he was given a warm welcome and free tickets to the show for the rest of the week!

But it was not just in America that the whites and the Indians intermixed. There were complaints in the local newspapers that Indians and white women had been seen walking arm in arm through Llandaff fields. If it was allowed in the Wild West, it certainly was not in Wales!

Buffalo Bill's Wild West Show crossing Canton Bridge, Cardiff, 1903. From the National Museums and Galleries of Wales (Welsh Folk Museum) collection

Bibliography

Elwyn T Ashton, *The Welsh in the United States,* Caldra House, 1984

John R Cook, *The Border and the Buffalo,* Crane and Co., Kansas 1907

Alan Conway (Ed.), *The Welsh in America – Letters from the Immigrants,* University of Wales Press, Cardiff, 1961

Davies, Eirug, *Y Cymry ac Aur Colorado,* Gwasg Carreg Gwalch, Llanrwst, 2001

William Davies Evans, *Dros Gyfanfor a Chyfandir,* Aberystwyth, 1883

Thos E Hughes and others (Editors), *The Welsh in Minnesota,* Mankato, 1895

A O Jones, *His Lordship's Obedient Servant,* Gomer, 1985

Bryn Owen, *Owen Roscomyl and The Welsh Horse,* Palace Books, Caernarfon, 1990

Jack Martin, *Border Boss – Captain John R Hughes, Texas Ranger,* Austin, Texas, 1990

Denis McLoughlin, *An Encyclopedia of the Old West,* Barnes & Noble, New York , 1995

Joseph G Rosa, *Wild Bill Hickock, The Man and his Myth,* Kansas University Press, 1996

Daniel W Williams, *Lecture to Montana Pioneers* (copy in Gwent Archives)

Peter Wood, *The Sully Kid,* ZBN, 1982

National Library of Wales (Owen Roscomyl Letters no. 9 – Owen Arthur Vaughan and article from *The Nationalist* 11, 22, December 1908, 7-12)

**Wales within your reach:
an attractive series at attractive prices!**

Titles already published:

1. Welsh Talk
Heini Gruffudd
086243 447 5
£2.95

2. Welsh Dishes
Rhian Williams
086243 492 0
£2.95

3. Welsh Songs
Lefi Gruffudd (ed.)
086243 525 0
£3.95

4. Welsh Mountain Walks
Dafydd Andrews
086243 547 1
£3.95

5. Welsh Organic Recipes
Dave and Barbara Frost
086243 574 9
£3.95

6. Welsh Railways
Jim Green
086243 551 X
£3.95

Also from Y Lolfa...

BLACK MOUNTAINS
David Barnes
The recollections of a South Wales miner – an extraordinary tale of suffering and survival.
0 86243 612 5
£6.95

THE DYLAN THOMAS TRAIL
David Thomas
A guide to the West Wales villages and pubs where Dylan Thomas wrote and drank.
0 86243 609 5
£6.95

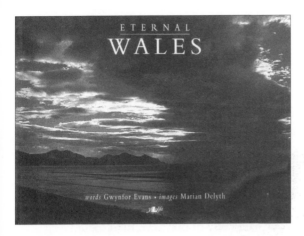

ETERNAL WALES
Gwynfor Evans & Marian Delyth

Beautiful, coffee-table book with unforgettable images of
Wales; text by Gwynfor.

0 86243 363 0

£24.95

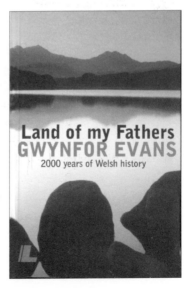

**THE LAND OF MY
FATHERS**
Gwynfor Evans
Lucid, masterful,
comprehensive,
passionate – and
essential history of
Wales.
0 86243 265 0
£12.95

The *It's Wales* series is just one of a whole range of Welsh interest publications from Y Lolfa. For a full list of books currently in print, send now for your free copy of our new, full-colour Catalogue – or simply surf into our website, **www.ylolfa.com**, for secure, on-line ordering.

Talybont, Ceredigion, Cymru SY24 5AP
e-*bost* ylolfa@ylolfa.com
gwefan www.ylolfa.com
ffôn (01970) 832 304
ffacs 832 782